JOB INTERVIEWING

Innovator of the Prestigious JOHN D. SHINGLETON AWARD for Outstanding Job Placement Research

INTERVIEWING

FOR COLLEGE STUDENTS

JOHN D. SHINGLETON

Printed on recyclable paper

VGM Career Horizons
a division of *NTC Publishing Group*
Lincolnwood, Illinois USA

Library of Congress Cataloging-in-Publication Data

Shingleton, John D.
    Job interviewing for college students / John D. Shingleton.
        p.   cm.
    Includes bibliographical references.
    ISBN 0-8442-4173-3 (pbk.)
    1. Employment interviewing.   2. College graduates—Employment.
I. Title.
HF5549.5.I6S368   1996
650.1'4—dc20   95-19411
                                                                                       CIP

Published by VGM Career Horizons, a division of NTC Publishing Group
4255 West Touhy Avenue
Lincolnwood (Chicago), Illinois 60646-1975, U.S.A.

6 7 8 9 0 ML 9 8 7 6 5 4 3 2

CONTENTS

2. Preparing for the Interview 49

5. The Offer   107

About the Author

John D. (Jack) Shingleton is a well-known career consultant and author in the fields of business, industry, government, and education. As Director of Placement at Michigan State University for over 25 years, Mr. Shingleton has appeared on the NBC Today Show and the CBS Morning News to share his expertise on human resources. His experience, made popular in part through his weekly career column in the *Detroit Free Press*, has also been sought in the creation of several television documentaries.

While at Michigan State University, Mr. Shingleton founded the Collegiate Employment Research Institute and *Recruiting Trends*, which he continued to co-author for 17 years. In recognition of his professional contributions, the Midwest College Placement Association (MCPA) named its annual outstanding research award for Mr. Shingleton. He also wrote many years for the National Association of Colleges and Employers (formerly named the Collegiate Placement Council) *Journal* and received its Outstanding Professional Award.

He currently is a member of the Board of Trustees at Michigan State University.

ACKNOWLEDGMENTS

I am especially grateful to the students and employers with whom I have worked in this field of career planning and placement. They are too numerous to mention specifically, but they have taught me much that is included in this book.

A special pat on the back to Patrick Scheetz, my successor as Director of the Collegiate Employment Research Institute, who is the leading researcher on employment trends for new college graduates in the United States, in my opinion. He is also current author of *Recruiting Trends,* an annual publication of the Collegiate Employment Research Institute. We still consult regularly on college student employment matters, and I find him most knowledgeable.

Thanks also to Betsy Lancefield, Associate Editor; Constance Rajala; and Kathy Siebel of VGM Career Horizons who also have contributed to this book.

Thanks also to my wife, Helen, for her suggestions and editing.

John D. Shingleton

PREFACE

So many graduating seniors, faced with leaving college and entering the world of work, are concerned about what to expect when they begin interviewing for their first job after college. Some realize the importance of the interview, some don't. Regardless, the interview is a turning point in their lives. As with any adventure, no one quite knows what to expect and how to cope with it.

This book covers the job interview from A to Z and can enhance your job potential considerably by helping you understand what you are looking for and how to get it.

Graduating from an institution of higher learning puts you in a special group in terms of what your future can be. Of course, what it can be and what it will be are two different things. You have the educational background and have been provided opportunities to gain experiences that will serve you well in the future.

The problem many seniors have when entering the job market lies in not recognizing they are in a very competitive situation. Employer representatives receive countless resumes, interview on several campuses, and talk to many candidates before making a decision to hire a person. In the more desirable companies, the employer may screen resumes and interviews of anywhere from 10 to 100 or more candidates seeking a position in the company.

Very often the difference between the person hired and the person rejected is not who is the better candidate but who is better prepared for the interview. Careers can be made and lost at that point alone. You need to spend the time and effort that will enable you to be better prepared than the competition. Recognize this and you will enhance your employability considerably. Above all, there is a job for you. You must believe that. Approach the interview with that in mind, for confidence is a part of the successful interview.

The issue before you now is to present your education and your experiences in the best way possible to those employers who have an interest in a person with your qualifications. Having so many credits, courses, or degrees doesn't necessarily add up to getting the position or career path you seek. You must be able to present your abilities, knowledge, insight, and personality in a way that will maximize your potential to find the slot that best suits your needs.

Being able to understand the importance of the employment interview and then to present yourself through your interviews in a successful way opens the door for infinite possibilities. The skill with which you handle the interview can have a tremendous impact on how successful you are in your job.

There is an art to the successful interview. Take the time to understand the importance of the interview. This book speaks to helping you maximize your potential when you interview for a position. Plan your interviews and give them a lot of thought — don't just drift with the current and let chance determine your future. Successful interviews can lead to successful lives. Work affects you socially, psychologically, physically, mentally, and economically. The job interview is the gateway to the world of work. Make the most of it. Good luck.

John D. Shingleton

To the memory of my mother and father.
Their values are the cornerstone of my life.

CHAPTER 1

The Concept of the Interview and Its Importance

An interview is the crown jewel of a job campaign. If you don't convert employment interviews into job offers, all other efforts are wasted. You make it or lose it in the interview. Thus it is of utmost importance that you prepare properly for the interview. This requires careful analysis of your past achievements, your current situation, and your anticipated preferences. Set aside the time to fix this information clearly in mind before you begin interviewing.

Advance Planning

Among the details needed before a job interview are a summary of your academic preparation, your prior work experiences, a description of the career you expect to pursue, the general category of organization you would like to join, and the preferred geographical area for your desired work.

Before pursuing prospective employers and getting interviews, other preparation is also needed to conduct an effective job campaign. Among the steps necessary for this achievement are: creating a creditable resume, researching various employers that may interest you, understanding the job market and your competition, clarifying your financial expectations, identifying the specific employers you want to interview, gathering all the information you need to sell yourself effectively, and identifying your references. Also important is an understanding of the various sources to obtain interviews, i.e., the placement office of your school, faculty contacts, friends who know of job leads, and a variety of other sources. You will, in addition, want to prepare a log of your interviews so you can check the status and results of those interviews at any given time.

Fundamentals

Preparation for the interview consists of three fundamental components. First, you must know yourself—your pluses and minuses—very well. And more important, you must be able to articulate who and what you are. Part of the preparation for an interview should include practicing your answers to certain questions.

Second, you must know your prospective employer and the anticipated job opening. You should know as many details as possible about the employers and the jobs you are seeking: the product line, profitability, organizational structure, employment locations, reputation of the employer, and the potential for advancement. The more knowledge you have about an employer, the more you can command the interview. You also can tailor your answers to questions the prospective employer is asking.

Third, you must know your competition and your bargaining position. To assume you have all the answers and qualifications that will guarantee you a job puts you at a great disadvantage.

It is much better to assume there will always be someone better prepared and qualified. This will make you try harder. Being knowledgeable about the whole job search strategy can greatly enhance your hiring potential.

Self-Evaluation

When asked what was most difficult for man, Diogenes answered "To know one's self."

When conducting a survey of employers across the country, I asked the question "What advice would you give new college graduates on the threshold of seeking a job?" The most frequent responses fell into the "know yourself" category. In my experience counseling students through the years, the one consistent problem for many was identifying the jobs that would best suit their interests, strengths and weaknesses, likes and dislikes, and their personality. If you are in this category, don't be surprised; you have plenty of company. This is due in no small measure to our highly structured, complex, and overly protective system of education. Throughout our lives we are defined by things like grades, financial status, and academic requirements set by others.

Now is the time when you must shed the cocoon of youth and come to grips with your true self. What do you really want from life? How do you expect to achieve *your* objectives? At no time in your life is this more important than when you are seeking that first job after graduation. Now comes the time when you must ask "What do I have to offer?"

Suddenly, you experience an identity crisis. The question "Who am I?" at once becomes a major question. How do you handle it? You think through the whole process and work out your thoughts. As a suggestion, write down your answers, if that will help. You will slowly discover the bits and pieces that are the true you. It's important that you are objective and honest with yourself.

Interviewing as an Art

Interviewing has been termed by some as an "art," primarily because there are many different ways to create a positive impression. Basically, the underlying rule of thumb is to "be yourself." This will help you have confidence and avoid later getting in awkward positions through being other than what you are or saying what you are not.

No one style is better than others assuming you adhere to the basics of courtesy, cleanliness, and professionalism. For example, if you are quiet and shy, don't try to be the life of the party, simply to impress the interviewer. An outgoing personality in most jobs can be an advantage, but the thing to do is to build upon the strengths of your style. In this book you will find many ways to build upon those strengths.

Strategies as You Begin Your Senior Year

If you haven't already explored your various career options, begin to do so immediately. Unfortunately for many seniors, this is "catch-up" time, but having an idea of your targeted career areas and possible routes for attaining them will greatly enhance your chances for successful interviews. Procrastination is one of the greatest inhibitors to getting a job—too many graduating students have faced this negative attribute and lost. Admittedly, procrastination is an easy option for career planning and has resulted in serious consequences for the person who is so inclined.

Concentrate on getting a job. Take advantage of all the opportunities your educational institution offers for exploration of job opportunities. Examples of these services include job fairs, job campaigning workshops, career seminars, occupational testing, career counseling, campus interviews, cooperative education programs, career planning classes, employer presentations, alumni contacts, vacancy bulletins, professional associations, meetings, and placement programs. Newspapers, magazines, and journals sourcing employment information can be found in *Business Publication Rates and Data* (Standard Rate and Data Service). Periodical indexes are another possibility, including the *Wall Street Journal,* which has its own career information publication. Reference directories such as the *Encyclopedia of Associations* can provide information on companies, executives, and organizations in your areas of interest. Interest can also be a source of job opportunities for those who can access it.

Much of this information is available in your institution's library, and some colleges and universities have career resources centers.

Positive Attitude

Finally, from the beginning of your interviews, develop a positive frame of mind. This is *very* important.

Keep in mind that you have spent 16 or more years of your life in preparation for this career you are willing to offer an employer. You made a considerable financial investment in education to reach this stage of your life. You are willing to offer a substantial portion of your future time (2,080 hours per year based on a 40-hour work week) for the mutual benefit of your employer and yourself. This is not a small offering!!

The employers, on the other hand, must hire employees who allow the organization to function properly. Both of you need one another.

All the preparation you have made will be for naught, if you come across as lacking confidence and displaying a lack of potential for doing the job the employer needs accomplished. Many graduating college seniors underestimate their experiences and abilities to do a given job, so don't let that happen to you. Put time and effort into knowing yourself, and you will be surprised at the reservoir of talents and abilities you possess.

Self-Assessment

Self-direction based upon self-evaluation is the key to focusing on knowing yourself and relating this information to your career aspirations. Self-evaluation can also lead to greater fulfillment of long-range career goals. Taking the time to think about the important things in your life is significant. Determining what you want to do with your life compared to the skills you have, your interests, your economic needs, and your personality also are very important. This is often neglected during career planning. Too frequently, people drift with the current of events, and thus they do not realize their life goals because they yield to procrastination and lack self-direction. Repeatedly, people simply depend upon the actions of others rather than shaping a purposeful and deliberate course of action for their own careers.

Begin by assessing your marketable skills. You will be surprised at the skills you possess. Try this simple procedure. List all the *specific* tasks you accomplished during current or former jobs you held. Highlight those tasks that you completed most competently. Also, list the tasks you achieved with medium and low competence. Follow this with a list of your personal capabilities, and include personal observations. Be specific when preparing this list.

Next, list factors in your life that are very important to you. Include long-term goals, career objectives, salary needs or expectations, geographical preferences, environmental choices, large or small employers, personal relationships, and other related matters.

Next, analyze your interpersonal skills, shortcomings, and strengths. Include likes and dislikes. When preparing this list, be as objective as possible and remember the words of poet Robert Burns: "Would the Lord the gift to give us to see ourselves as others see us." You may want to ask your friends to help with this task, because you cannot afford to be too biased!

Testing for career alternatives can be a very valuable experience for some students when determining their interests, aptitudes, and attitudes. Specific tests vary in their objectives, but most colleges and universities have counseling programs for this purpose. My advice is to seek a career adviser at your college or university who might help you identify specific tests that might be best for you (e.g., the Self-Directed Search Career

Assessment helps students focus on their strengths and weaknesses). Then have the professional counselor help you interpret the results of any tests. These can then be related to general career interests and occupational preferences. The SIGI Plus test is another computerized career decision-making program designed to guide students through a career selection process.

Generalist vs. Specialist

The academic discipline you pursued during college may or may not have a bearing on the field of work you will enter following graduation. Students don't always enter into employment in their college major. You will hear that job opportunities for specialists (i.e., engineers, nurses, accountants, etc.) are better than employment prospects for generalists (i.e., liberal arts, social sciences, and communications arts majors). The fact is, there are opportunities for both. Academic programs from all areas have for decades been producing new college graduates who become both generalists and specialists, and practically all these graduates found good opportunities and satisfying lives. Make up your mind that there is a career out there for you and you will find one.

A proper attitude is half of the battle for anyone wanting a successful job campaign. As a daydream, think of the famous attorney Joel Hawes' statement, "You will be whatever you resolve to be. Determine to be something, and you will be something. 'I cannot' never accomplished anything; 'I will' has wrought wonders."

Setting Priorities

It is crucial in the process to identify things that you really like to do and rank them in order of preference. The process of prioritizing your desires will reveal your value system to a large extent. Your value system should play a major role in your decision making.

Here are some questions that might trigger a few answers for you:

Review your entire education, examining the courses you've taken, books you have read, and papers you have written.

Itemize your work experiences: part time, full time, temporary, and volunteer.

Note your hobbies, sports, activities, avocations, and geographical preferences.

What are your hopes, wishes, and desires in the long run?

Do you have certain activities that you can't pursue all the time nor make into an occupation, but certain jobs or locations could provide you with the opportunity to participate in these hobbies on a part-time basis and improve your quality of life?

Do you like to work inside or out of doors?

How important is money to you?

As you work on this exercise, more ideas, thoughts, and concepts will evolve. Avoid dealing in generalities, such as "I want to be successful," "I want to make money," and "I like people." For example, being successful usually comes after you have chosen an occupation and pursued it for several years. Select an academic field of study or occupation you enjoy and are capable of handling. Chances are you will then be successful.

One last word on this subject. Most people underestimate their potential contributions and the possibilities they have to offer. Put time and effort into knowing yourself and you will be surprised at the reservoir of talents and abilities you discover. The secret is to channel these talents and abilities properly.

Developing an Interviewing Strategy

When developing an interviewing strategy, it is important to recognize that an employment interview is a *two-way* discussion, and you should feel on equal footing with the employer. Your responses will be much better if you act on this premise. Being defensive and subordinate will not enhance your bargaining position.

Understanding the Job Market

In order to have a successful interview, it is important to understand the job market for the various disciplines prepared today by colleges and universities and to react to the current market in a realistic way in order to get positive results from your interviews.

The nature of the job market has changed in recent years and finding the "right" job is becoming more complex. I say, "right job," because there are enough jobs available for most college graduates who choose to work; finding the one that fills one's particular needs is another story.

The market has more recently been reported as "improved" and "encouraging," which is good news. One of the reasons is that the national unemployment rate has improved. This appraisal is accurate in one sense, however, it can be an oversimplification of a rather complex issue, when it comes to finding a position commensurate with the expectations of the graduate. Thus, while there are jobs for most graduates, many new degree recipients do not know how to thread their way to rewarding jobs with a career potential.

Generally speaking, students in the technical areas: sciences, accounting, medical occupations, and business fields, have a more favorable market for their services, although there have been temporary pockets where supply exceeds demand, as evidenced by the changing demand for geologists and nurses, for example.

Those graduating in such disciplines as biological sciences, fine and applied arts, foreign languages, communications, natural resources, and the social sciences will find jobs available, but the competition will be greater for positions in these fields.

One of the most overlooked areas of employment (in most disciplines) is sales. Sales and marketing careers have unusual characteristics that are common to all industries and are in demand universally.

The economics of the job market being as dynamic as they are, the results are a wide range of salary offers for new college graduates depending upon their academic major, total number graduating in a given year, and the graduate's education and prior career-related work experiences. (See the following Charts A, B, and C.)

It will be some time before we again reach the heights of the pre-1990 era, pointing out that there have been fundamental changes in the way employers conduct business. Computers, voice messaging systems, automated technologies, and a whole different style of management have combined to totally revolutionize the work environment.

Chart A

Bachelor's Degrees Expected — By Gender of Recipient

Year	Total	Men	Women
1991–92	1,136,553	520,811	615,742
1992–93	1,153,000	521,000	632,000
1993–94	1,165,000	526,500	638,500
1994–95	1,179,000	528,000	651,000
1995–96	1,198,000	541,000	657,000
1996–97	1,201,000	540,000	661,000
1997–98	1,204,000	543,000	661,000
1998–99	1,232,000	541,000	691,000
1999–2000	1,196,000	541,000	655,000
2000–2001	1,198,000	544,000	654,000
2001–2002	1,210,000	552,000	658,000
2002–2003	1,227,000	561,500	665,500
2003–2004	1,248,000	572,000	676,000
2004–2005	1,264,000	581,000	683,000

Source: National Center for Education Statistics, 1994. *Projections of Education Statistics to 2005.* Washington, D.C.: U.S. Department of Education, Office of Educational Research and Improvement, p. 61.

Chart B

Estimated Demand by Field of Study—For Bachelor's Degree Graduates of 1995–96

Academic Majors	Estimated Numbers	Percent of Total
FAVORABLE SUPPLY/DEMAND RATIO		
Business and Management	270,476	22.6%
Engineering and Engineering Technologies	81,733	6.8%
Health Professions	65,057	5.4%
Computer and Information Sciences	25,885	2.2%
Physical Sciences	17,877	1.5%
Total Graduates	461,028	38.5%
COMPETITIVE SUPPLY/DEMAND RATIO		
Education	113,845	9.5%
Protective Services	19,874	1.7%
Mathematics	15,582	1.3%
Other Subject Areas	13,830	1.2%
Architecture and Environmental Design	9,226	0.8%
Total Graduates:	172,358	14.4%
VERY COMPETITIVE SUPPLY/DEMAND RATIO		
Social Sciences	141,217	11.8%
Psychology	66,947	5.6%
Communications and Related Technologies	57,949	4.8%
English Language and Literature	57,922	4.8%
Visual and Performing Arts	49,037	4.1%
Biological and Life Sciences	45,263	3.8%
Liberal and General Studies	33,913	2.8%
Multi/Interdisciplinary Studies	21,763	1.8%
Public Affairs	16,851	1.4%
Agriculture and Natural Resources	15,942	1.3%
Home Economics	15,703	1.3%
Foreign Languages	14,655	1.2%
Parks and Recreation	8,903	0.7%

(Continued)

Chart B

Estimated Demand by Field of Study — For Bachelor's Degree Graduates of 1995–96 *(continued)*

Academic Majors	Estimated Numbers	Percent of Total
Philosophy and Religion	7,933	0.7%
Area and Ethnic Studies	5,631	0.5%
Theology	4,985	0.4%
Total Graduates:	564,614	47.1%
GRAND TOTAL — ALL FIELDS	1,198,000	100.0%

Source: Estimates by John D. Shingleton and L. Patrick Scheetz, Ph.D., Michigan State University. Grand total of bachelor's degree recipients from *Projections of Education Statistics to 2005*, published by the National Center for Education Statistics, U.S. Department of Education, Washington, D.C., 1994, p. 61

Chart C

Estimated Starting Salaries for New College Graduates of 1995–96

Academic Majors	Starting Salary Expected
BACHELOR'S DEGREE GRADUATES	
Chemical Engineering	$41,910
Mechanical Engineering	$36,785
Electrical Engineering	$36,361
Industrial Engineering	$34,601
Computer Science	$33,745
Nursing	$30,981
Civil Engineering	$30,733
Geology	$29,549
Chemistry	$29,407

(Continued)

Chart C

Estimated Starting Salaries for New College Graduates of 1995–96 *(continued)*

Academic Majors	Starting Salary Expected
Accounting	$28,863
Physics	$28,150
Financial Administration	$27,638
Mathematics	$27,429
Marketing/Sales	$25,277
Agriculture	$24,944
General Business Admin.	$24,429
Hotel, Restaurant Institutional Management	$24,332
Human Resources Management	$23,650
Education	$23,356
Natural Resources	$23,215
Social Science	$23,058
Retailing	$22,639
Advertising	$22,089
Communications	$22,079
Human Ecology/Home Economics	$21,567
Liberal Arts/Arts and Letters	$21,335
Journalism	$21,046
Telecommunications	$21,030

ADVANCED DEGREE GRADUATES

MBA	$40,693
Masters	$37,012
Ph.D.	$39,846

Source: Estimates by John D. Shingleton and L. Patrick Scheetz, Ph.D., Michigan State University.

Numerous clerical, administrative support, and middle management positions have been eliminated to allow businesses and industrial organizations to show profits and governmental agencies to balance budgets. At this point, it appears that personnel staffing has been cut sufficiently to enable some employers to begin replacement of experienced personnel with new college graduates.

What Employers Say

A recent survey by the Collegiate Employment Research Institute indicated that the economic climate of the nation topped the list of factors influencing job opportunities, followed by improved financial health of organizations, organizational restructuring, and low attrition rates among current employees.

Employers participating in the survey encouraged fresh graduates to be realistic in their career expectations and consider entry-level positions to enhance and develop job skills. Also suggested was the acquisition of additional skills including foreign languages, computer expertise, or accounting, which could supplement marginal credentials. A willingness to relocate was also cited as a factor for increasing job prospects.

Employers also stated that hiring employees to work throughout a lifetime for one organization is a theoretical ideal, but it is not a realistic expectation. Change is constant and preparation for change is a necessity. Restructuring and downsizing are continuing, so employers can only maintain recent hires as long as there is work.

When advising graduates on the best places to consider for job opportunities, employers recommended working for small- to medium-sized companies, niche sectors of the economy, contract employers or agencies, geographical pockets where the economy is especially good, and pursuing openings in international/overseas areas.

Employers also said that the most common mistakes made by new college graduates when interviewing with prospective employers were lack of preparation by the student in researching the employers and self-preparation for the inter-view. To quote one employer, "They try to shoot from the hip, and it doesn't work."

Growing Occupational Areas and Employment Markets

The growing occupations and employment categories in the current job market for new college graduates are computer-related occupations, engineering, sales and marketing, accounting and finance, and medical and health care services. An analysis of schedules of employers visiting campuses indicates that the following is a list of the occupations and employment categories recruiters are seeking:

- Computer systems occupations including local area network positions, management information systems, information analysts, personal computer programming, computer information systems specialists, and computer science assignments;

- Engineering including electronics, chemical, electrical, civil, construction, mechanical, software, manufacturing, industrial, design, environmental, systems, and engineering technology;

- Accounting and finance including financial analysts, operations management, logistics management, management change specialists, and human resources management;

- Sales and marketing, retail management, technical sales, store sales trainees, buyer trainees, telemarketing, etc.;

- Medical and health care occupations including nurses, nurse practitioners, physician's assistants, physical therapists, rehabilitation specialists, occupational therapists, speech therapists, vascular technologists, biotechnologists, food scientists, etc.;

- Environmental fields including waste management, environmental management, waste disposal systems specialists, etc.;

- Sciences and mathematics including chemistry, chemical processing, and actuarial;

- Economic and community development including community planning, hazardous waste, transportation planning, environmental health and safety, and legal administration;

- Communications and telecommunications including wireless data, satellite, switching systems, digital signal processing, etc.; and

- Hotel, restaurant, and leisure field occupations.

Source: L. Patrick Scheetz, *Recruiting Trends 1994–95*. Michigan State University.

Be Confident

How, then, do you develop a frame of mind that enables you to have the confidence to ace the interview? There are several things to realize:

1. The employer has a need to fill a position in order to make the organization function. The employer is going to considerable lengths to hire someone who can best fill that need and it's to the employer's benefit to hire. Presumably, it will cost the employer money if a good candidate is not hired. Thus, it is imperative for you to recognize that you can help the employer, given the opportunity.

2. You have made a considerable investment already in preparing for employment. For example, you have spent at least 16 years of your life getting an education so that you can be productive as an employee. You have taken specialized courses to help you produce for the employer. You have made a tremendous financial investment in preparing for this employment. That is no small contribution. You are prepared to put all of your education, experience, and know-how into the job. Just as the employer will make a significant contribution to your well being, so too, will you be contributing to your employer's success and accomplishments.

3. Remember that the interviewer will do all he or she can to make the job opportunity as attractive as possible should you be the desired candidate for employment. By the same token you must make sure all your positive points are well known so the employer can evaluate you in the best light possible. You must also collect all the information you can about the employer to help yourself match your qualifications with the needs of the employer and make a decision should an offer be extended.

4. Above all, think positively when going into the interview.

As you can now tell, your strategy is to be well prepared. Rest assured the interviewer will thoroughly review your resume and any company materials before this session. If you have thoroughly strategized before the interview, your bargaining position will be enhanced tremendously, and, in turn, your chances of being hired will be increased significantly.

Be Prepared

If you are planning on entering a job interview without a great deal of preparation, you are selling yourself short. There are some who can "wing it" but most of us add to our competitive edge by doing homework before the interview.

The ultimate goal of an effective job campaign is landing a position that matches your likes and interests. The objective of the interview is to provide a mutual understanding between you and the employer that is the main vehicle for the job offer.

Interviews vary depending upon the interviewer and the stage of development in your job campaign. For example, the first interview may be a screening session, so an initial applicant pool of many prospects is screened to a desired few. This is usually accomplished by a member of the employer's personnel department, especially if you are a walk-in candidate. Or this task may be completed at a campus placement office. Sometimes, if you represent a specialized discipline such as accounting or engineering, the initial interview will be conducted by an accountant or engineer.

Usually, the next interview is performed with staff from the employing department, normally at the site of the employer's choosing. This is often referred to as an on-site or plant interview. When you go to an interview, remember the following tips:

1. Always take resumes with you when you have an interview, just in case the person talking with you does not have one. At the plant visitation, you may have several interviews with numerous individuals or groups of employers. Be prepared to take psychological tests during these visits, if the employer resorts to such selection techniques.

2. When preparing for the interview, be sure to check all available materials you can obtain on the employer — the annual report, brochures on the product line, locations of facilities, profitability, organizational structure, etc. If you have an opportunity to know the selection criteria before the interview, and this information is frequently made available by the employer in their advertisements and job descriptions, study them carefully to organize your presentation. If you can talk with some current employees of the organization beforehand, this could also be helpful.

3. Be ready to ask questions (covered more completely in Chapter 2).

4. Be properly groomed. Make sure your clothing is consistent with the general attire of employees working for the organization. Good personal hygiene is an absolute.

5. If you have to present any materials in the interview, be sure they are prepared and presented professionally in an attractive manner.

6. Arrive on time. Allow for possible parking problems. Do not arrive a half hour early — five minutes before interview time is about right. If a restroom is nearby, check your attire and grooming beforehand.

7. If the interview takes place at lunch or dinner, avoid alcoholic beverages and smoking as a general rule.

Remember, the interviewer has probably had a lot of experience interviewing. He or she has probably been trained in interviewing techniques, questions to ask, and factors necessary to make the basic decision: Do we want to further consider or hire this individual?

During this interviewing process, you should be thinking in the same vein as you analyze the employer: Do I want to work for this employer, and do I want to proceed with further interviews should they be necessary? Or, have I decided not to work for this organization?

Thinking about all these points and selected issues in advance is important if you want to be prepared for the interview. With such preparation you will also be more confident, more relaxed, and better able to present yourself in the best light possible.

Be Smart

A great deal of effort goes into the job hunt—preparing the resume, networking, researching, letter writing—but nothing is as important as the interview. Many people put considerable energy into the job search factors mentioned above but not enough thought and effort into the interview itself.

You can improve your interviewing skills with practice and by using some common sense "smarts." There are a few key points to remember:

1. Relax. Avoid last minute rushes. Advance preparation breeds confidence.

2. Be yourself. Trying to put on a false face during the interview won't work. You will also feel more comfortable answering questions when you are honest and sincere in your responses.

3. Market yourself. All of your responses should relate your qualifications to the job available. Fifty percent of the conversation should be yours. Do not be reluctant to initiate subjects that will enhance your chances.

4. Prepare for the interview by knowing what your responses will be to certain questions. Also, identify questions you will want to ask. Build a bridge between the job and you.

5. Avoid controversial subjects. Don't belabor a cause in which you may have an interest if it doesn't fit into the flow of the interview.

6. Be sure all of your good qualities are known before you end the interview. Some interviewers miss important qualifications in a candidate and it behooves you to make sure that doesn't happen. Have your accomplishments firmly in mind before the interview so you can relate them to the job.

7. Don't speak negatively about your peers, former employers, faculty, or other employers. Keep an upbeat and positive approach to all you say in the interview.

8. End the interview with a course of action. Make sure you have closure. This can be when next the interviewer will contact you, when the interviewer will arrange an on-site visit, even rejection. Also, be sure you know what your next step is and when you are to take a certain course of action. In short, summarize what you and the interviewer have decided.

9. Send a thank you letter to the person(s) who interviewed you.

Group Interviews

Group interviews can be intimidating to the fresh college graduate but they need not be. A few things to keep in mind are:

1. Take your time in responding to questions.

2. Be sure to talk to all of the people interviewing you. Do not focus on one person and ignore the others.

3. Envision the group interview as a one-on-one interview and don't be reluctant to ask questions and give opinions.

4. Occasionally, there will be one interviewer in the group who is trying to impress the other interviewers rather than ask prudent questions. Some may be trick questions. Don't

let this ruffle you. Take your time and answer in a polite way and by all means avoid being hostile.

Be Careful

The results of an interview are predicted on more than an exchange of words. For example, what you say is important, but how you say it can be equally important. Do you show enthusiasm, energy, and interest? These can be shown in *how* you respond to a question as well as what your words are. Your attire, grooming, cleanliness, body language, posture, walk, handshake, eye-to-eye contact, choice of words, speech characteristics, breath, cooperativeness, and courtesies you extend, *ad infinitum* — all go into the hopper before you land a job.

Interviewers not only seek to hire people; they also screen out candidates. Exclusive of all your skills, education, and experience, negative factors that will screen you out of a job are:

1. Poor appearance
2. Poor attitude
3. Indications of dishonesty
4. Bad-mouthing others
5. Lack of enthusiasm
6. Tardiness
7. Excessive aggressiveness
8. Suspected instability
9. Body odor
10. Questionable eating or drinking habits
11. Indications of lack of dependability
12. Indecisiveness

Do all recruiters put the same value on these factors? No, it varies with the person. You can reduce the wash-out risk by avoiding the above during the interview. Many interviewers put more emphasis on screening *out* candidates than screening *in,* so avoid those factors likely to eliminate you—and thereby enhance your chances of getting hired.

There Is a Job for You

The economy plays a major role in the employment of college graduates. The recession of the early 1990s delayed the employment of many seniors entering the world of work. There was no question that many did not have jobs at graduation, though within six months after graduation most of them found employment, although not always in their disciplines. Certainly those who continued to work hard at finding employment were eventually successful. Many employers cut staff during this period, mainly experienced personnel. This creates a bubble in the manpower pipeline and eventually vacancies created will be filled by graduating seniors.

Certain employer categories thought there was a surplus, in some areas, including automotive and mechanical equipment companies, electronic and electrical equipment manufacturers, aerospace and its components, and banking, finance, and insurance industries. These fluctuations receive considerable media attention, but don't conclude there are no jobs. When interviewing it is important to remember that you are one person looking for one job. There is always one good job out there for you. Never give up on looking for the job you want—regardless of the economy, what the media say, or the number of rejection slips you gather.

Even if the first position you accept is not all you expected it to be you always have the option of changing. Turnover for technical graduates averages about 5 percent in the first year and nontechnical graduates are about double that. Over a three-year period turnover averages about 20 percent for technical and 30 percent for nontechnical personnel.

Industries vary greatly in turnover, with aerospace leading. Others with higher than average turnover on the nontechnical side are the hospitality, communications, hospital, and retailing industries. Turnover varies greatly by industry, employer, and economic conditions, however, and you must judge each organization on its individual characteristics.

Opportunities for Face-to-Face Interaction

In face-to-face interaction, you stand to make your greatest impact. Recognize this and make the most of any opportunities that present themselves. In face-to-face contact, you can convince a prospective employer that you can be a valuable employee. The impression you create can be the most important part of the employment process.

Is the first impression important? You bet it is! Some say, the decision to hire a new graduate is made in the first 5 minutes of the interview. Maybe so, but don't count on it! Having said all that, don't let your opportunities rest on the first 5 minutes. The interpersonal factors developed during the entire course of an interview are very important. While different people have different styles that can be successful, you have to decide on the best style for you.

As an initial suggestion, don't try to be someone you are not. Be yourself and try to be flexible enough to interrelate with the interviewer's style. Avoid confrontational responses. Concentrate on the questions and make sure your responses put your best foot forward. Not all interviewers are good ones, so make sure that you highlight all your experiences and qualifications for the job prior to completion of the interview. While your resume will list your qualifications, your face-to-face interaction supplements and should promote your strengths. Avoid stating your qualifications that cannot be supported factually.

Face-to-face interaction is the time to ask questions that help you understand all the elements of the position. Plus it also assists you in making the decision of whether you want the job should it be offered. It helps the interviewer know if you are interested in the position and indirectly provides other relevant information for a meeting of the minds. Remember, you are there to learn about the position as well as help the interviewer learn about you as a good candidate for the position.

Recognize that the face-to-face interview is the single most decisive stage of the job hunt. All your previous efforts to communicate your education, work experiences, career preparation, and other qualifications have been exerted to place you in a favorable position for this moment in time. Basically, the interview has a three-fold purpose. First, the employer wants information about you—the "real" you—that cannot be covered in resumes and credentials. Second, the applicant wants more information on the employer that cannot be provided through brochures, word-of-mouth, and reputation. Third, a bridge of contact needs to be established between the two. Understanding this process automatically places you in the proper frame of mind. It helps you participate as an equal partner in a two-way, give-and-take session, where both sides mutually enlighten one another. Many graduating college students do not see this point, so they make the mistake of "all take and no give" (and some even make the opposite error).

Pre-Interview Thoughts

There are some basic tactics that should be planned early in your senior year to make sure you have the proper foundation for successful interviews, assuming you have not already done so. We will arrange all of these elements later, but there are a few items you should have well in hand, if possible, before the interviewing process begins.

1. Make sure your degree requirements are confirmed at the beginning of your senior year, thus eliminating the possibility of last minute surprises that can thwart your graduation and cause subsequent difficulties.

2. Alert those faculty, associates, former employers, and others that you may give as references when you apply for employment. Give each potential reference a copy of your resume so they will have an updated picture of your background, experiences, and education.

3. Try to identify your short- and long-term career goals, so you have a solid sense of direction that is consistent during

interviews with prospective employers. This helps when formulating your responses to the interviewer's questions as well as indicating you know yourself, your career alternatives, and how to get there.

4. Identify a network of friends, associates, faculty, former employers, and relatives. Let them know you are embarking upon a job campaigning effort and would appreciate any suggestions or help they could offer. A copy of your resume and a personal call would also be appropriate.

Recruiters . . . What You Can Expect

You can expect to encounter a wide range of recruiters. Most campus recruiters are full-time employees of the employing organization, but not necessarily full time in recruiting. Depending upon your major, you may be interviewed by personnel department staff or by specialists from the various units within an organization, i.e., engineering, accounting, marketing.

Age, skill, personality, and experience vary greatly. Expect all kinds of interviewers and interviews. Neither will follow a standard pattern. There may be cases where the student has to carry the interview to keep the discussion on a track that brings out the best in a candidate, though most of the time the recruiter will lead the interview. The personality of the recruiter is often the personality of the employer, but not always. Do not predicate your further interest in a company on the campus recruiter. On the other hand, you can be fairly certain your on-site interviews will be representative of the personality of the employer.

Some recruiters will have a narrow understanding of the total personnel needs of the organization. This is often the case when recruiters represent only certain departments or functions of the company. Most recruiters, if not knowledgeable about the needs in the company for a person with your discipline, will refer your resume to the appropriate departments for perusal. Usually, the larger employers have a campus representative who can speak to all the personnel needs.

Generally speaking, campus recruiters are skilled at interviewing. While they don't always make the final decision as to who is hired, and where, they play a prominent role in referring and recommending candidates. Never underestimate their importance to your being hired, however.

Getting the Right Interview

For those students at schools where excellent placement programs exist, the student should take advantage of all the opportunities afforded by those services. On many campuses this can be a primary source of interviews for most students.

Career Planning and Placement Offices

When using the career planning and placement office, take advantage of the full range of interviewing possibilities. First, learn the system. Too often students do not take the time to learn about the many employers who seek applicants from their schools. The students were "too busy" to review bulletins on employers interviewing on campus and the jobs they were attempting to fill. The senior year is a busy time for most graduates; it is nevertheless necessary to take the time to talk to the employers when they are visiting on campus. This process is much more efficient than most other recruitment methods. It also provides an opportunity to have face-to-face contact with employers who might not otherwise be available to you for interviews.

Take advantage of the career library to learn more about employers. Visit with career advisors, as they may hear of leads not listed in placement bulletins for employers visiting campus. Attend career fairs so you can personally talk with employers. Any time you can make contact with employers on an individual basis is always better than approaches by telephone or letter.

Finally, be sure your credentials are on file at the placement office at all times during your senior year. Employers periodically contact placement offices for credentials of graduating students, prior to campus visit or to fill immediate openings. Review bulletins and other information on employment opportunities distributed by your college placement office.

The Hidden Job Market

Contrary to what many people believe, most entry level jobs for graduating seniors are not filled by interviews with recruiting representatives on campus. Studies indicate that of those employers *visiting campuses*, 42 percent of those hired were hired through this process in their companies. They hire about 12 percent by write-in resumes and applications. Don't be misled by these statistics, however, because most employers do not visit campuses to recruit for various reasons—too small, not enough demand, too costly, etc.

Thus, the graduating senior must not ignore the Hidden Job Market that literally is all around. This applies in good times and bad, winter and summer, all over the country.

Advertised and posted jobs, especially for government jobs, constitute a large portion of the positions available, but there are still many other options.

Exploiting the hidden job market takes creativity, innovation, and a special kind of initiative to generate the many opportunities available through this method. Here are a few:

Personal Contacts

Probably more people find jobs from personal contacts than through any other method. Do not be reluctant to let people know you are looking for a job. Their contacts include friends, family relations, neighbors, faculty members, college alumni, and business associates of the aforementioned individuals. Attending conferences and professional meetings also can be an excellent source of leads. This is a form of networking to inform people that you are looking for employment and/or to ask advice on whom they would recommend you talk to about setting up an interview. This is also referred to as "pyramiding"—contacts with one individual to gain an interview with another.

Help Wanted Advertisements

These provide another source of job opportunities. National newspapers such as the *New York Times,* the *National Business Employment Weekly* of the *Wall Street Journal,* the *Chronicle of Higher Education,* the *Los Angeles Times* and the *Chicago Tribune* are examples of excellent sources and can provide many leads. If you have a geographic preference for Denver, for instance, you could subscribe to a Denver newspaper. Using this method can help you zero in on a particular area. Blind advertisements, without the employer's name mentioned, contrary to some people's opinion, can lead to good opportunities. Some are recruitment efforts for lower level commission sales positions or related assignments.

Membership Lists

Such helpful references from associations are another source of leads to contact (See Appendix B). One of the best is the *National Association of Colleges and Employers Job Choices,* which lists many major employers seeking college graduates throughout the nation. Other journals, professional magazines, and directories can provide a vast number of leads.

Employment Agencies

Sometimes helpful, but experience suggests that they are not the best source of job opportunities for most seniors—other than in the highly technical fields. If used, I recommend you use employer fee paid agencies only.

"Contract" Employers and Agencies

Increasingly popular, such organizations have provided satisfactory job options for some graduates. When hired by a contract employer, you are hired by one company at their salary and benefit program and they then sell your services to another company.

Contract Employment

Not very long ago, many college graduates would not interview with "contract employers." Under contract employment arrangements, students are interviewed for temporary and part-time employment through a "contract employer or agency." This employer is then hired by a permanent employer. The numbers of new college graduates entering contract employment are increasing, because contract employment reduces costs for salaries and benefits to the permanent employer. Also, many jobs today do not have a long duration before completion, thus contract employment reduces overhead compared to hiring permanent employees with benefits on a regular payroll.

While it is not practical to go into all the details of contract employment, this employment option can sometimes lead to full-time, permanent status. I recommend that graduating students not overlook this avenue of employment. This is especially true for those graduating students who are having difficulty finding permanent employment.

It is important when interviewing with contract employers that you understand precisely who your employer is and the conditions of your employment.

Contacts Made through Summer Employment, Internships, and Part-Time Employment

All are excellent leads for getting the right interviews. In fact, many employers use these precedents to recruit many of their permanent employees.

Professional Organizations

Almost all associations often offer placement services to their members. Many also sponsor career fairs, job campaigning seminars, and career conferences.

Federal and State Government Job Lists

The Civil Services regularly list their job openings. Be prepared for a slower employment process when applying to government agencies versus business or industry. Many excellent career opportunities are available to new college graduates interested in government employment.

The United States Employment Services (U.S.E.S.)

This has not been a highly productive source for most graduating college students, but sometimes seniors get jobs through these services.

You must be a self-starter to get the right interviews. Determination and aggressiveness are required. You must be prepared for negative responses—but not let those responses get you down. It only takes one "yes" and you are on your way! This is one area where persistence pays off. Identify the right targets and your chances of hitting the bullseye are greatly enhanced. And remember, the more contacts you make the greater your chances for success. Finally, remember that arranging interviews takes time, effort, and money to do it properly. Prepare yourself mentally and financially—and schedule the time necessary to do it properly.

Computer Databases

Another very good source of interviewing opportunities is computer databases. Depending upon the techniques used and the costs of these databases, their potential can be rated from very good to poor. This is a fairly recent innovation using personal computers to bring candidates and employers together.

Computerized Resume Services

The computerized resume service is one direct marketing option sold by numerous agencies. The process of registering for one of these services is very easy. Each applicant completes a resume profile including career interests, prior work experiences, academic achievements, salary requirements, special skills and abilities, and geographical preferences. Interested employers search the database using the job description for each available employment opportunity. By refining the selection criteria, employers can reduce the available applicants to a limited number for interviews.

Most in demand by prospective employers using these databases are any applicants in high visibility academic majors, high tech fields, women applicants in predominately male-dominated occupations, and minority applicants in almost any demanded job category. For an applicant pool containing several of these applicants, employers will pay very well.

This recruiting method is used as merely one source in a total recruitment program. Most employers still visit college campuses for conducting interviews, rely on current employees for referrals, and sometimes resort to printed advertisements to encourage more applicants.

The primary costs for these databases are paid by the prospective employers. These fees will vary from $50 to $100 per search, or $1,500 to $3,000 for unlimited searches during a year. To be listed in one of these databases is normally free or inexpensive for new college graduates, usually costing from $10 to $50 for two months, six months, or a year. Experienced candidates or those seeking higher starting salaries may have to pay a slightly higher fee.

Also note, however, that some employers measure worth of resumes in these databases using the following criteria: grade point averages, prior career related work experiences, campus leadership positions attained, and degrees received. If your academic record and prior work experiences are marginal, your probability of being selected from one of these databases is not very good.

Examples

Several examples of these databases include kiNexus, Resume-Link, the Restrac Resume Reader, Jobhunt, the College Recruitment Database, ABRATRAK Applicant Tracking System, AMA-Applicant Management System, ATS-Applicant Tracking System, ATS-III, Jet*Scan national databank, Compu-Source, and Ross Data Services. More are arriving in college placement offices each month. Other systems were discontinued because of financing problems, technical difficulties, or lack of national acceptance. It might be a good idea to inquire into the financial solvency of these resume services before paying any fees.

Computerized Job Listings

Job listings are accumulated in databases as another technique marketed by computer vendors. As one example, the National Employment Wire Service (NEWS) database collects employment opportunities from local newspapers and distributes this information via computer modem to college placement offices. By using this source, prospective employers can be identified from numerous regions around the country, but keep in mind that you must send the employers a resume and cover letter, and then visit these prospective employers in person, possibly at your own expense, before you can be hired. So, do not become too enthusiastic about sending resumes to every matching job listing.

Examples

Besides the NEWS system, other examples include the Career Advisory Network, Peterson's Connexion system, Datext business databases, and DIALOG databases. Before entering any of these databases, review their success history. Ask questions about the numbers of individuals hired previously from each. Learn about the employers utilizing each source and the academic majors pursued by these employers. Also make yourself aware of the costs involved—to you and the prospective employer, and any potential commissions on your starting salary.

Although these databases can be quite helpful for identifying potential employers, the tasks of interviewing with the employer and landing the job are still your responsibility.

Internet

There is a job search revolution taking place through the use of "Internet." When using this technology, employers have re-engineered and automated their recruitment and hiring functions so you, the student, can gain access and more easily communicate with organizations regarding available job opportunities.

In Joyce Lain Kennedy's new book, *Hook Up, Get Hired,* she has written detailed descriptions of the methodologies for gaining access through Internet to unparalleled employment opportunities. This book is for the person who wants to use the latest technologies for resourcing the job market. She outlines procedures for identifying jobs through the best net bets, bulletin boards, other modem connections, jobs reached through newsgroups, sources on Gopher, listings available on the World Wide Web (www), telnet, and e-mail.

Those seeking information on small business opportunities, government job postings, listing resumes in employer and job-bank databases, and many other sources of job prospects should read this book. It also lists permanent, part-time, temporary, and contract jobs in a most comprehensive directory. See Appendix C for more information sources on Internet. It is certainly the wave of the future and will be worth examining.

Computerized Placement Office Systems

Contact your college or university placement office to determine their automation capabilities. Some placement offices register graduating students and alumni via computer terminals, and referrals from these databases often yield additional interviewing opportunities. It is also possible to access these databases with your own personal computer. Register with them when appropriate, and use them to identify job prospects related to your background and preferences.

This area of cultivating contacts is really in the developmental stages and has to be refined to be totally efficient. It is a source of contacts, however, and can be helpful to certain candidates in selected disciplines.

Almost any area of employment a student plans to enter today requires computer skills of varying degrees. If you have these skills, be sure they are discussed in the interviewing process, as such information will enhance your chances of winning the job.

*Generating
Interviews
through Mass
Mailings*

For most graduating seniors, blind mass mailing of resumes to employers is not very efficient unless you have special skills and have an exceptional educational and experience background. Where the supply/demand ratio heavily favors the candidate, doors can be opened via this method, but even then, persons with the outstanding and exceptional characteristics would do better to more precisely target their prospective employers. A survey made a few years ago showed that of employers visiting campuses, about 10 percent of the total graduates hired were "write-ins."

Many college recruiters hire very few via submitted resumes. It simply is not an efficient way to recruit. Large corporations receive tens of thousands of resumes in the mail each year; one organization received over 300,000 resumes through the mail, unrequested. While any staff would like to spend more time reviewing resumes, most of the paper will be reviewed for not more than five to twenty seconds. That means thousands of hours of valuable time has been wasted when that time could have been spent much more productively.

Also, mass mailings work better with smaller employers than larger ones, simply because of the difference in volume received by each. Small, entrepreneurial employers are apt to be more receptive to the inquiring candidate than those in the Fortune 500 ranks.

Marketing Yourself

Excellent marketing skills really make a difference when interviewing with prospective employers, and you can develop those talents much more than you might think with a little planning and some effort on your part.

One of the first superficial liabilities for most first-job-seekers is a lack of experience. Yet, college students have far more experience than they realize. For instance, you have energy, experience dealing with people, part time and summer work experiences. Regardless of the menial labor required by the job, you understand the value of work and the techniques required to work well with others. Identify the skills you have learned from athletics, club memberships, travel, and hobbies. Relate to the job you are seeking your college course work, papers you have written, and the experiences you have gained from 16 or more years of education. Try to avoid developing an inferiority complex about your lack of experience. There are thousands of jobs on the employment market that can use a person with the above-mentioned experience.

There are numerous statistical ratios that could be helpful when developing your marketing strategy. There are proven methods for generating sales of products and services. You can use the same strategies when selling yourself. The following chart demonstrates one example:

Developing leads of 100

Generates 25 possible prospective employers

Leading to 15 definite prospects

Generating 10 interviews

Yielding two offers

Resulting in one job acceptance

This method of marketing your talents demonstrates that you must be able to accept rejection and move on. As you proceed, minimize your weaknesses and maximize your strengths. Talent is always important in any job-seeking effort, but recognize that it is not always talent alone that lands the job. Talent plus timing is often the combination that breeds success.

Your Own Marketing Plan

At the foundation of successfully marketing your skills is your marketing plan. First you must prioritize your interests, likes, dislikes, goals, and abilities so you have a well-defined career objective. Then schedule your interviews with those employers whom you think can best help you reach your objective. Contacts can be generated from friends, lists, directories, placement offices, libraries, and professional organizations.

Then prepare for the interviews as covered in "Developing an Interviewing Strategy" earlier in this chapter. Achieve a positive attitude toward your recruiter and the interview outcome. It helps if you remember that every rejection brings you closer to acceptance since there is a definite ratio between the number of rejections and the final acceptance. While this ratio varies for each individual and the employers involved, sooner or later the acceptance factor emerges.

Appearance, also mentioned earlier, is a critical factor when marketing yourself. Many interviewers make their decisions regarding future consideration for employment within the first five to ten minutes of an interview. In fact, your appearance conveys a message about you that words cannot convey. Appearance becomes especially important in initial interviews since it opens the doors for further interviews and more detailed analysis of your credentials.

Dress is an extremely important part of your overall appearance, so do not be reluctant to spend a few dollars on your clothing and accessories. Emphasize quality. Most students have limited financial resources in their senior years, but here is one place where a small investment can make a major difference.

Some basics to remember:

1. Pay attention to your grooming, (i.e., clean fingernails and proper hair care). Don't keep your hat on! (I dislike having to say this but I have witnessed some students do this.)

2. For most business jobs, wear conservative, classic clothing in darker tones. Medium blues, navy, and gray are best bets for men; blues, black, dark brown, and burgundy are good choices for women.

3. For men, suits are best, although when finances won't allow it, a well-pressed sports coat with proper matching pants is acceptable. Most employers recognize that recent college graduates are not loaded with money, but they do expect you to be neat and clean. For women, classic suits

are always acceptable; dresses are very good, providing an opportunity for a little more creativity. Avoid extremes in skirt lengths and bright colors. Sweaters and skirts are marginal at best.

4. Shoes make a difference. Be sure your shoes are shined. Leather is best. For men, brogues do well and loafers are acceptable with black or brown recognized as the best colors. For women, classic pumps are always proper with a 1½–2 inch heel. Black, navy, and brown are the best colors.

Another fundamental of a good interview is to place yourself mentally on equal footing with the interviewer. Don't feel inferior or that the interviewer holds all the cards. Obviously, don't be too aggressive and kill your job chances immediately. But do sit upright in your chair and speak clearly.

Generally speaking, the interviewer and the candidate should each speak about 50 percent of the time during the interview, although this varies. Make sure your best points are known to the interviewer and all your questions are answered before terminating the interview. Keep your liabilities to yourself. Avoid negative comments about former employers, faculty, or your college. When appropriate, use positive statements about past employers or faculty.

Listen carefully to the interviewer. Concentrate on the questions asked and think before you provide answers, especially when replying to open-ended questions. And do not be reluctant to ask questions. Remember, a good interview is a two-way street.

Be sure your best strengths are mentioned but keep your weaknesses to yourself unless specifically encouraged to comment on them. Then be truthful. If questions are asked regarding your use of drugs, answer honestly. Most larger companies require physical examinations that include drug testing.

In spite of all of the cautions mentioned above, it is important that you be yourself. Trying to be someone that you are not has numerous pitfalls.

Finally, follow-up after the interview is another chance to market yourself. A good follow-up letter reminds the interviewer of your visit and reinforces your quest for the job. Often he or she will be interviewing many candidates, and sometimes individual candidates tend to blur in the interviewer's mind. If your follow-up letter doesn't bring a response in ten days to two weeks, follow up with a telephone call to reinforce your interest in the position.

The Resume as It Relates to the Interview

The resume is an important tool when preparing for the job interview. This document conveys all your experiences, academic preparation, and relevant information pertaining to your qualifications. It makes you think about your prior accomplishments, your methods of achievement, and your future career prospects. Properly prepared, it gives you an outline to assist you immensely in the interviewing process.

In fact, the greatest value received by anyone who prepares a resume may come from the review it gives you before the interview. It helps you place in chronological order your activities, restoring experiences that you might not consider prior to an interview without having prepared a resume. Depending upon the type of resume you prepare, in addition to placing your facts in chronological order, it will help you recreate your experiences, provide reasons for selecting your career paths, identify your achievements, and fit your skills and abilities with the employer's needs.

Having prepared your resume, you are provided with a database from which you draw your answers to questions during the interview. The resume refreshes your memory. The resume also can be the focal point for the interview, depending upon the employer's style of interviewing. In most cases, it complements the interviewing process. Obviously, great care and effort should be taken to assure that the combination of the resume and the interview present you in the best possible way.

A poorly prepared resume—poor punctuation, misspelled words, incorrect grammar—can obviously eliminate the possibility of an interview. Should you get an interview in spite of a poorly prepared resume, it could start you off on the wrong foot with a prospective employer. As image-making tool, the resume should be in concert with the professionalism of the interview. Having a strong resume can make the difference in your selection for a position. Treat it as one of the most significant documents in your job campaign.

There are many uses for a resume other than providing a picture of your background. For example, preparing a resume helps you organize your education, experiences, and objectives when seeking career alternatives. It can be given to references so they can respond better to inquiries about you. Faculty or summer employers may not always know as much about you as you think.

A resume should be left with individuals whom you contact when networking. It can open doors that you can't reach through personal contacts. A resume can project your qualifications in a positive manner. It can serve as the basis for an interview. It can be helpful when completing employer application forms, and may become part of your permanent record with an employer.

When preparing a resume, be brief. Chances are, initially it will be scanned quickly. Use action words that succinctly tell your story. Appearance of the resume is important. Good quality, off white or beige paper is a safe bet. Usually one page is sufficient, although two pages are acceptable. Do not crowd the margins, and, of course, make sure the spelling and grammar are proper. Layout is important for emphasis and overall appearance.

Preparation Is a Major Part of the Interviewing Process

Whenever you enter a negotiating situation, it is important that you determine and maintain firm objectives. Career opportunity should be foremost in your thinking. Be realistic in your bargaining position and be honest when evaluating your market value.

At the same time, be optimistic about your career goals. There is usually some give and take before final agreement is reached. On those items fixed in your mind as extremely important and not negotiable, do not compromise. Minimum salary required to exist might be an example. Keep in mind, however, that you are just getting started in a career and opportunity is more important than starting salary.

Before going into an interview, try to understand the employer's bargaining position and their general criteria for hiring personnel. Knowing the employer's alternatives can make a major difference in your expectations.

Be sure to cover all the basics when negotiating—starting salary, benefits, expected travel, starting date, moving expenses, holidays, housing, and training. Avoid getting into highly specific discussions of these items until it appears that the employer is interested in hiring you. You will never be in a better position to negotiate than at this point.

When the employer makes a job offer, there is a desire among many to accept the offer on the spot. Absolutely avoid this temptation! Be sure you understand the offer. Ideally, try to get the offer in writing, including all the details.

After getting an offer, if it doesn't meet your expectations, then you may want to shift your requirements to sometime in the future. For example, if the starting salary offer doesn't meet your expectations, ask if a raise is possible within three or six months, assuming your work is acceptable. Again, get this part of the agreement in writing. You may want to accept a negotiated offer on the telephone but be sure it is confirmed in writing.

Recent graduates having numerous interviews often receive several offers. Before accepting an offer, complete all your scheduled interviews, even though most employers will not wait more than a few weeks before withdrawing a job offer. However, if you have a legitimate reason for an extension, be sure to discuss it with the employer. After reviewing all your potential opportunities, accept the most attractive option.

Do not renege on an acceptance once you have made a deal. Nor should an employer renege on an offer and acceptance. The National Association of Colleges and Employers has established a Code of Ethics recommended for employers and graduates that is fair and equitable. This code is available in most placement offices; read it before interviewing.

Check List for Fringe Benefits

Fringe benefits are an important part of the compensation package. Some counselors advise not to worry about fringe benefits, especially when you are first starting out on a career. Wrong! Benefits can be a substantial part of what you receive for your work, running as high as 30 to 35 percent of your salary, depending upon the employer. Not all employers offer the same benefits. Some pay the cost of all benefits; more often the benefit costs are shared between employer and employee.

Here are some of the common employee benefits offered by many employers and the percentage of companies offering each type:

Common Employee Benefits Offered

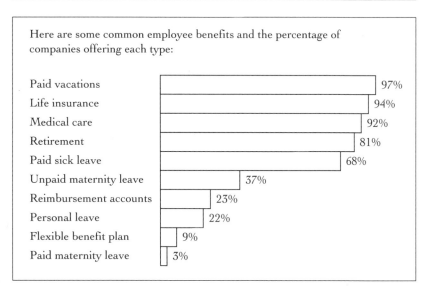

Here are some common employee benefits and the percentage of companies offering each type:

Benefit	Percentage
Paid vacations	97%
Life insurance	94%
Medical care	92%
Retirement	81%
Paid sick leave	68%
Unpaid maternity leave	37%
Reimbursement accounts	23%
Personal leave	22%
Flexible benefit plan	9%
Paid maternity leave	3%

Source: Bureau of Labor Statistics, 1989

Following is a list of benefits and who pays for those benefits:

Benefit	Who Pays
1. Retirement benefits.	Usually employer
2. Life insurance.	Usually employer. Employee may pay supplemental costs.
3. Medical insurance.	Costs usually shared between employer and employee. Look into this option carefully so that your particular needs are met.
4. Vacation.	Usually two weeks per year for the first 3 to 5 years. Three weeks after 3 to 15 years. Four weeks after 15 years.
5. Holidays.	Employer paid. Usually 8 to 10 days per year.
6. Sick leave.	Varies greatly with company.
7. Dental insurance.	Costs usually shared. Not always offered by employer.
8. Disability insurance.	Costs usually shared. Not always offered by employer.
9. Tuition assistance.	Most large companies pay all or part of tuition, books, etc. Usually employer only pays for courses related to work.
10. Child care.	Cost usually shared, but not all employers provide child care though some do.
11. Bonuses.	Cash awards based on performance or suggestions.
12. Commission.	Cash awards based on volume of sales. Remuneration can be 100% commission or combination of salary and commission.

13. Draw.	Weekly or monthly amount paid regularly against commission sales.
14. Stock purchase.	Employers offer employee stock at price below market value.
15. Matching savings plan.	Employers match employees' savings up to a certain percentage of salary.

Work Schedules

"The old order changeth making way for the new." This adage is particularly applicable to the work schedules recently (mainly since the early 1980s) adopted by many employers. The 36 to 40 hour work week is still the standard for most employers, but this is rapidly being shortened, lengthened, compressed, and sliced into many different formats.

Following are some of the work schedules enjoyed by some employees. These plans vary greatly among employers and even departments within companies.

Compressed Work Week

By adjusting the hours per day work, employees work 40 hours per week in 4 days (10 hours per day) and eliminate one work day.

Part-Time Work Day

Employees work one quarter, one half, or three quarter time and are paid accordingly. Some employers offer benefit packages to these employees on a pro-rata basis. Others do not.

Flex Time

Hours are arranged by mutual consent of employer and employee. This alternative cannot be arranged in many organizations because of the nature of the work. With those employees with whom it is possible, it is becoming popular. Can be ideal for working parents.

Shared Jobs

Usually two people work half time each to fill a full time job. Requires good cooperation between employees. Ideal for working parents.

Temporary Work

Very popular with most employers. Allows employer to meet peak demand periods of production. Benefits limited if for shorter than 6 month periods.

Home-Based Work

Work is performed at home. Ideal for jobs such as editing, telephone sales, and direct sales.

Overtime

Employer usually pays time and a half for overtime over 40 hours. Many salaried positions graduating seniors would fill require more than 40 hours per week for which there is no additional pay over 40 hours. Job candidates are advised to find out during the interview what the expectations are with regard to pay for overtime, especially if the job entails considerable overtime.

Salary Negotiations

Doing your homework on your marketability and the employer's salary policies can pay handsome dividends. Research the average salaries for people with your experience and education. Such information can usually be found in the career planning center, the placement office, the National Association of Colleges and Employers' Salary Survey, the Collegiate Employment Research Institute Survey, and other published surveys. Not all college graduates start at the same salary. In fact, some majors start, on average, at twice the salary of other majors. Graduates of some of the better known schools sometimes command higher salaries than graduates from lesser known schools. Employers in the same business have a wide range in their salary schedules. Certain industries traditionally pay more than others. By doing your homework you should have a fairly good idea of the salary you should receive from a given employer.

When negotiating remuneration, be sure to include all the factors—salary, vacation time, bonuses, medical benefits, employer paid benefits and employee paid cost for benefits, expenses, salary review periods, dental and optical insurance coverage, and other forms of remuneration.

Timing and having all the facts in hand so you understand your bargaining position are important. Leave the discussion on salary to the interviewer unless it's not brought up—in which case you gracefully broach the subject. Some employers advertise their salary ranges to candidates, in which case you know in advance the general parameters. Still, there often is room for negotiation and employers do bargain, depending upon their bargaining position and company restraints. Remember, though, that once on the job your potential for negotiating further salary adjustments is reduced considerably and your bargaining position has eroded.

Timing

Regardless of the endeavor you are pursuing in the world of work, timing is important. Thus it is with interviewing and finding success in the job market.

For a new graduate just finishing college, control over timing is difficult. For example, a person graduating at a time when there are massive layoffs in business and government will experience limited job opportunities. Others who graduate when the economy is booming and employers are on a hiring binge will find excellent job opportunities. Few college graduates have much control over the date of their graduation.

Recognize a difficult job market situation when you face it and realize that you must work harder to generate interviews. Prepare for more rejection letters and seriously consider the possibility that you may have to settle for something less than what you expected. When anticipating a tight labor market, you will want to start interviewing early in your senior year and certainly not less than six months before you expect to begin working.

When the economy is healthy, be sure to complete all your interviews with the desired employers, since you may receive several offers. You will want to be sure to settle on the best one. Being alert to the job market will give you the sense of aggressiveness needed for landing a good job offer.

Risk-Taking

Recognize from minute one that the decisions involved with a job search require risk-taking in varying degrees. You will constantly be positioned to make decisions that can have long-range implications for your life and your happiness.

During the interview, you will be faced with decisions that will have an element of risk. So recognize that this is the nature of the business. It behooves you then to be flexible and agile when responding to questions in the interview that can impact on whether you will or will not be considered for employment. Advance career planning can reduce risk considerably, but no amount of career planning will reduce risk entirely.

I mention this as an element of the interview to forewarn you so you will not forego opportunities that you might pass by simply because of the "risk" you might see in a situation. The less risk you choose to take, the less opportunities you will have. Successful careers have always been associated with risk. Those who avoid risk often are destined to be "low person on the totem pole."

Chances are that you will have more capabilities and can perform in a position of greater responsibility than you think. Thus, when faced with a risk decision, whether it be with a minimum or maximum potential for failure or gain, be sure you look over all of the factors involved and remember that there can be a high risk when *avoiding* risk. This is especially true in career decisions. I cannot tell you what to do when faced with risk decisions except to make you aware of the consequences of the right or wrong decisions. My experiences with many college graduates is that they err in opting for certain risk decisions when the consequences are not nearly as risky as they assume. Most opt for stability and certainty. Only you can decide what is best for you.

Job Hunting for People with Physical Disabilities

Personal contact is the key here. As Placement Director, I made a special effort to assist "handicappers" and found that invariably when they had a chance for a face-to-face interview for a job, their chances of employment increased considerably. Admittedly, not all employers accepted the idea, and this approach required that the candidates be more aggressive than they normally wanted to be. We found that placement personnel could be helpful if they would assist individuals with disabilities to get onto interviewing schedules. The on-campus interviewing procedures vary by institution, but do not be bashful about getting the director of placement's assistance in getting you on the schedule if you have the proper credentials.

Laws have changed dramatically, and employers, especially those who have hired individuals with disabilities, find that these individuals are a resource that has been much overlooked in the past and one that can provide solid, dependable, and loyal employees.

Marketing yourself plays a major role when convincing an employer that you can do the job, so do your homework on the requirements of the job and identify the variety of skills and talents you have to offer.

Sometimes it is necessary to accept a position where you are underemployed to prove yourself. This applies also to people who do not have disabilities. It may be advisable to accept a part-time or temporary position to demonstrate that you can perform in a given job. Do not be reluctant to accept a lower-level position. The main objective for any new college graduate is to get into a regular work environment.

One very good source of career information is the National Library Service for the Blind and Physically Handicapped, Library of Congress, 1291 Taylor St. N.W., Washington, D.C. 20542. Keep in mind that many job seekers have some disadvantages when pursuing employment opportunities. The secret is to identify those jobs where your disadvantages are minimal or of no importance when performing the job.

I have heard many employers say after hiring an individual with disabilities that they are among the best they have employed.

CHAPTER 2

PREPARING FOR THE INTERVIEW

Normally, 50 percent of an interview will consist of questions about you and your background, experiences, interests, likes and dislikes, motivations, attitudes, skills, and abilities. You must be prepared to answer numerous questions centering on these points. To best answer these questions you must know yourself—and these questions can help you in this respect.

Questions, Questions

If you feel you don't know your wants in a career, start the process by asking yourself some basic questions. For example:

1. What would I like to do?
2. What motivates me?

3. What am I prepared to do?

4. If asked, "What is your objective in this interview?" how would I answer the question?

5. How important is money to me?

6. Where would I most like to live?

7. Which employers would make my career most enjoyable?

8. Do I plan to obtain additional education?

9. When can I begin working?

10. What are my assets and liabilities?

11. Why do I want this job?

Start with these questions of yourself, and add as many other questions as you can think of. Take time, write your answers. This process will help you during the interview. You will come across as knowing yourself and your objectives. Contrast this with the person who flounders on some answers to these questions; that interview isn't nearly as successful.

Students often are confused when answering real life questions after being exposed to a multitude of philosophies, lifestyles, and opinions while attending college. Crystallizing all this input in advance will help you know yourself and enhance your outcome for a successful interview.

Questions You Should Be Prepared to Answer

Each interview is a unique experience and the range of differences among interviews is infinite. Personalities, chemistry between people, type of organization, time differences, interview types (campus, on-site, etc.), technical compared to non-technical interviews, interview setting, nature of job, qualification emphasis of the job opening, and experience of interviewer are just some of the factors that make each interview different from any other.

Nevertheless, employment interviews generally have much in common. Knowing this, you should be aware that proper preparation can enhance your chances for landing the job. Provided below is a partial list of questions you should be prepared to answer, even though you may not experience all of these questions in any one given interview. Rehearsing these questions in advance can make your answers more explicit and should add to your confidence during the interview.

Your answers should always convey professionalism, accomplishment, honesty, diligence, and grace under pressure. Whenever possible, highlight your productivity and efficiency. *How* you answer questions can make a big difference in your success.

In this context, then, here are some of the questions and comments you should be prepared to answer:

1. Tell me about yourself.

2. Why are you interested in this position?

3. Why should we hire you?

4. What do you consider your strengths and weaknesses?

5. Why did you select this university for your academic preparation?

6. Why did you choose to major in _____?

7. How were your college expenses financed?

8. What is your overall grade point average?

9. What is the grade point average in your major?

10. Do you have any geographical restrictions?

11. What goals have you established for yourself?

12. What do you do in your spare time?

13. What are your salary expectations?

14. Have you ever used drugs?

15. Do you have any physical disabilities that would impair your employment with us?

16. How did you like your last employer?

17. Where do you expect to be in five or ten years?

18. What do you know about our organization?

19. Tell me about the lessons learned in your internship, summer employment, co-op experience, etc.

20. What position in our organization interests you?

21. Are you willing to travel?

22. Have you changed your major while in college?

23. What qualifications do you have that would make you particularly qualified for this job?

24. How did you happen to apply for this job?

25. Do you feel you have attained the best scholastic record of which you are capable?

26. Tell me about your experience in the armed services (if applicable).

27. What are your plans for graduate school (if any)?

28. When could you make a visit to our plant site for further interviews?

29. When are you available for employment?

30. Have I missed anything?

There will be other specific questions, obviously, pertaining to your resume, education, and work experiences.

What Employers Say

Favorite Interviewing Questions

Employers responding to a *Recruiting Trends Survey* were gracious enough to share some of their better, favorite, and/or most often used interviewing questions. A few of the best are listed below, categorized according to personal background, skills and abilities, academic preparation, and other topics.

Personal and Motivational Factors

Please tell me about yourself. How would you handle rejection? Who or what had the greatest influence on your life? How would you describe yourself? What are some of the greatest personal challenges you have faced during your lifetime? What are some of your personal goals, and have you achieved them?

Skills and Abilities

What skills and abilities do you possess that will help make you successful in today's job market? Please discuss some of your past leadership roles and your accomplishments in them. Please describe a frustrating experience from school or work, and tell me how you dealt with it. How do you interact with people around you (i.e., leadership, communication, socializing, etc.)?

Why should our organization hire you? For you, what are some of the pros and cons of working on a team project? Have you ever supervised someone in a similar position with another organization? How would you describe your supervisory style? Who was the most difficult person you have ever dealt with, and how did you respond?

How did you organize your time in school, work, or play? What are your major strengths and weaknesses? What personal factors do you consider most important when evaluating yourself? In what organizational structure do you function best? What organizational techniques do you use on a daily basis to accomplish your academic, work, and social goals?

Please tell me about your communication skills, your personal skills relevant to work experiences, and your problem-solving abilities. Please describe your leadership style. What skills and/or special qualities do you possess for this job that would make you stand out from other candidates? How well do you work with others? What skills and abilities do you bring to this job? Please list three personal attributes that you would like to improve, and tell me any efforts you've made to make improvements in these areas.

What do you see as your greatest challenge when starting a new career? How would your friends describe you? What motivates you to put forth your greatest effort? In what areas are you working to improve? Who are two people you admire and respect the most, and why? What aspects of your job at the XYZ organization were most frustrating?

If you could create the perfect job for yourself, what would you be doing? What is special about you that you feel would make you an attractive candidate for our organization? How would others describe your weaknesses? How do you organize your time?

Career Goals and Objectives

What are your long range goals and objectives? How are you preparing to achieve them? What are your goals and aspirations for the next three years? five years? ten years? What are your short- and long-term goals? What are your standards of success/ goals for a job? Are you goal oriented?

Why do you think you would be good at this profession (sales, retailing, marketing, etc.)? Please describe your ideal job. Why are you interested in this industry/profession/occupation? What are your career interests? What work would you like to do that really interests you? In what environment do you want to work? What geographical location interests you most when working? Please tell me about your plans for the future. What is your timetable for achievement of your current career goals?

Do you prefer theoretical or practical problems? Why do you want to work for XYZ company? In this organization, where do you see yourself in five years? Please tell me five things about yourself that would make you an asset to any organization that hired you.

Extracurricular Activities and College Experiences

With what extracurricular activities have you been involved? Please tell me about your accomplishments in extracurricular activities. What have been your greatest challenges for improvement of a campus organization? What do you enjoy doing most? Please describe your most rewarding college experiences. Please cite examples of the challenges you experienced during your leadership positions with campus activities.

If you could relive your college experiences, what would you do differently? What changes would you make in your overall campus life? During your campus activities, what positions did you hold? What were your major responsibilities in these organizations? What did you like best/least about these positions? Did you have an opportunity to work as a member of a team? If so, please explain. What were some of the problems you encountered?

Hypothetical Questions

Are you creative? . . . I am writing a book entitled "101 Everyday Uses for the Common Red Brick." Can you give me five uses for the common red brick?

Please look at this photograph of an electronic gadget, because you would be working with others to enhance its capabilities. It operates a helicopter hovering over an ocean platform. What are some concerns that you would place on your checklist to consider before you started this project?

What could you see as the major objectives of this job? If you were hired by our organization, how would you identify the major roles and responsibilities of your new position?

What roles and responsibilities have you accepted in work, social, and other activities? What is your purpose in life? For what companies have you worked, and were they good or bad, and why? What have you admired in people who have previously supervised your work? What haven't you admired in these individuals?

In your opinion, what does it take to be effective in sales or marketing? What are your personal motivational techniques? How would you resolve conflict in a group situation? If you were given this assignment, how would you proceed?

Academic Programs and Achievements

Why did you choose this major field of study? Why did you choose your particular college or university? What were your favorite college courses, those you liked most? Least? Why? Please tell me about accomplishments in your academic program that are relevant to your future career goals.

What is your grade point average (GPA)? How do you feel about this? Should grades be used as an indicator of future career potential when an organization is considering new college graduates? What were your reactions to instructors or college faculty during your academic program? How would you relate your academic accomplishments to future career aspirations? How satisfied are you with your accomplishments in this academic program?

What electives did you take outside of your major? Why did you choose these courses? What was the most difficult aspect of obtaining a college degree? What are your academic strengths? What courses gave you the most difficulty? If you could, what changes would you make in your school's academic program?

Work Experiences

What prior work experiences have you had? What were your accomplishments in these prior work experiences? What were your most significant achievements? What problems did you experience while on the job? What would your last two employers say about you as an employee, either good or bad?

What projects were accomplished during your time on the job? How were these accomplished? What experiences did you have when meeting deadlines for project completion? Explain. What can you tell me that you enjoyed most about your previous job experiences? Least? Can you tell me about your toughest job assignment? Please tell me about a conflict situation and how you resolved it.

What life experiences have given you the greatest reward? What one experience proved to you that you would be a capable manager? Please elaborate on one of the work experiences listed on your resume. Please tell me about the duties/requirements of your last job. What did you see as your major strengths and/ or weaknesses on this job?

Accomplishments and Achievements

In addition to your educational and professional experiences, what else would you like us to know about you in order to make an appropriate decision? Please tell me about some of the accomplishments you achieved during college and which make you the proudest?

How did you finance your education? What are your greatest achievements at this point in your life? Of what accomplishments are you most proud?

Relocation/Travel

Are you willing to relocate? Do you mind traveling? How do you feel about relocating during a career with XYZ company?

Knowledge of the Organization

Why did you select XYZ company? Why do you want our training program over others? What are your expectations of the XYZ company? Why do you want to work in the position you are seeking? What attracts you to this industry? Other industries? Why are you interviewing with XYZ company? What do you know about our company? Who else are you interviewing in your job search? Why did you choose to interview with our company? What personal qualities do you bring to this firm?

Salary and Benefits

What starting salary do you expect as an employee? What company benefits are most important to you? How do you feel about an income made up totally of commissions? When comparing one company offer to another, what factors will be important to you besides starting salary? How important is starting salary to you when considering our company's job offer?

Questions You Should Be Prepared to Ask

Remember that an interview is a two-way street. You must look at the interview as an opportunity for the employer to gain information about you, but you must also receive information about the job and the employer. This is a very important point, but many graduating seniors fail to get all the information they need to make proper decisions during their job searches.

If your placement office provides workshops on interviewing techniques, attend them, especially if you have limited experience with the interviewing process. Make a list of any questions you want employers to answer *before* going into the interview. Memorize them. Make sure you ask these questions before leaving the interview.

Timing is also important when asking questions. For example, avoid asking questions on benefits or salary in the initial phases of the interview. Be aware of the approximate length of the interview, so you can get all your questions answered before the interview time has ended. This is especially true at the on-campus interview, since these sessions are usually 20 to 30 minutes long and a rigid time schedule is maintained. By all means, make sure your best points are known before you leave the interview. The interviewer will not always emphasize these points, so it behooves you to assume that responsibility. Obviously, different positions elicit different questions, but the following list includes some general questions you should be prepared to ask:

1. Who was the last person to hold this job, and what is he or she doing now?

2. Who will be my immediate supervisor? You should request an opportunity to meet this person during an on-site visit.

3. What are the possibilities for promotion?

4. What is the organizational structure, and where does this position fit in?

5. What is the extent of travel required on this job?

6. What are housing conditions in the surrounding geographical area?

7. What is the starting salary for this position?

8. What is the current financial condition of the organization?

9. Specifically, what will my duties be (if not already discussed)?

10. Do you have a training program for this position? If so, please briefly explain the program.

11. Are graduate degree programs available to employees in this position?

12. I am interested in this position. When will I hear from you regarding further action on my application?

Best Questions Asked by Job Applicants

What have been some of the *best questions asked of you* during your experiences with interviewing prospective job applicants? When listing some of the best questions asked of them by job applicants, employers provided several excellent examples. Their questions are categorized into the following groups: general topics, career motivation, anticipated job responsibilities, work environment, affirmative action, quality of work, personality factors, products and services, employment trends, measures of work performance, salary and benefits, and interview closure items.

General Topics

What is the financial stability of this company? What future changes do you see for this company? What direction do you see your company going in the future? Who are your competitors? How successful have you been with marketing your company's products? What plans does the company have for becoming more competitive in this industry? What is the biggest negative about your company? What makes your company different from others?

Career Motivation

Why did you accept work with this company? How long have you been employed with this company? Why do you continue to work for XYZ organization? What do you like most (or least) about your company? Would you want your son/daughter to work for this company too? What makes your association with this employer enjoyable? What are you really hiring me to accomplish? Graduating students are really wanting to get past the recruiting jargon to learn what is truly expected of them. Why should I take this job (or . . . work for your company)?

Anticipated Job Responsibilities

If I were hired by your organization for this position, what duties would I be performing? What will be expected of me in this position? How does my job fit with the mission of the organization, company performance, or profitability? How do you know when to hire additional staff? How much responsibility will I have? Why is this job important to you? What will I be contributing to the organization? What do you wish you knew about the company before you started? What would you change about this position, if you could?

Work Environment

What is your corporate culture? How would top management describe the corporate culture, and how does this compare with things in the organization as they really are at the lower levels? What were your personal experiences on this job? Will I be on a team, or in a group? How much freedom am I given to solve problems with my own methods? What help is available to me when my methods fail? Is this a new position? Why did the other person leave? What is your company really like?

Affirmative Action/Equal Employment Opportunity

What is the standard of living among minorities in your local community? What minority programs do you have?

Quality of Work

What differentiates your company from your competition? Do you get repeat business from your customers? What are the ethical and environmental philosophies of your company? What has been the history of turnover among recent hires in the company? What is this company's philosophy towards their employees? What is the relationship of this organization to the local community?

Personality Factors

What can I do with my education and training for your company? What values are sacred to this company? What would cause me to leave the company? How mobile can I be?

Products and Services

Has the company thought of going in the direction of xxx? What impact will the clean air legislation (or other current topic) have on the company? What impact did your recent service/change (or logo, product, market blitz, etc.) have on your business? What do you see as the biggest areas of needed improvement within the company?

Employment Trends

What significant changes has the company experienced in the past year? What are short- and long-term strategic directions of the company? What have been the successes (or failures) of the company? What is the company doing to change for success in this changing global economy? What are the company's goals for the future? What is the greatest challenge, from your perspective, that the organization faces during the next year?

Measures of Work Performance

How would you describe the most successful employees in your company? Can I expect opportunities for advancement with the company, if I work hard to prove myself? If I do well, what will I be doing in five years? How will I be evaluated in my job? How often will I be evaluated? Who supervises this position? What is the chain of command for this position? Where would my career progress from my first assignment? How does your company encourage their new hires to keep pace with advancing technologies? What characteristics do you possess that have made you so successful? What can I do within the first five years to help ensure my success within the company? What was your career path within the company? What feedback has been given to your company by recent new hires?

Salary and Benefits

What is the pay for this position? What are advanced educational opportunities with XYZ organization (MS, MBA, etc.)? May I someday invest in the company? What training would I receive if hired?

Interview Closures

How did I do? Do I get the job? How soon will I hear from you? What does your company want from successful candidates for this job? What would distinguish one candidate over another for this job? How do I prove myself and my commitment to the company? When would you want me to start in this position?

"Weeder" Questions Used by Employers

During campus interviews and plant visits, some recruiters ask "weeder" questions for the purpose of eliminating candidates who may not be appropriate employees for an organization. Potentially, every question asked in a thorough interview is a "weeder" question. Employers have shared some of their organizations' favorites.

1. General honesty and integrity: What is your academic major? Your overall grade point average? Why do you feel you are the best candidate for this position? What skills and abilities do you possess that would make you an ideal candidate for this job? Tell me when you have taken initiative and gone beyond what was expected. How would you describe yourself—assertive or behind-the-scenes—and why? When have you ever dropped the ball?

2. Educational background: Why did you choose this college or university? Why did you choose this academic major?

In what geographical location do you want to work? Why? Are you willing to relocate? What have you done to prepare yourself for a position with our company? Why should we choose you over someone else? Are you planning to attend graduate school? Why did you sign up for an interview with our company? How do your studies relate to the work environment in our organization?

3. Job preferences: Describe your ideal job and work environment. What are your career aspirations? What are your long-term goals and objectives? What do you think you will be doing with our organization five years from now? What opportunity are you seeking? What are the things that motivate you? Why do you want an assignment in . . .? Are you willing to travel? What are you hoping to avoid in a job? What assignments don't you like? How did you handle working with difficult co-workers? Tell me about a situation where you experienced rapid change. How did you handle it? How would you define a successful career? How will you evaluate the company you hope will hire you? How many hours do you expect to work on an annual basis? What makes you think you will like a career in this field?

4. Earlier work experiences: How do you feel about your previous supervisor? What experiences have you had when working with multiethnic co-workers or other employees? Do you have experiences working with persons who have a different background from your own? What were your favorite working hours? Do you have experiences in organizing work activities (decision-making, leadership roles, etc.)? What was your favorite earliest work assignment? What was your least valuable work experience? Describe your work style. How do you think your previous supervisors would answer our reference checking questions?

5. Technical questions: If confronted with this problem, how would you approach and begin to solve it? Do you prefer working alone or on a team? Define cooperation. Typical job assignment scenarios may be given and applicants may

be asked what they would do. The applicant's thought processes may be analyzed. How do you prioritize? How do you solve problems? Are you well organized? Do you handle pressure well? What do you do when pressed for a decision? Tell me how you have convinced someone on an approach or idea verbally.

6. Prior research of the organization: What do you know about our company? Why are you interested in working here? What identifies this company apart from other organizations? What do you think makes a person a success in this industry? What do you expect of the company that hires you? Do you have relatives currently employed by our company?

Some employers may not like "weeder" questions. In interviews with representatives of these organizations, questions generally focus on past performance and build on the applicant's qualifications. In this way, the best overall applicant can be chosen.

Source: *Recruiting Trends 1993–94*. East Lansing, MI: Collegiate Employment Research Institute, Michigan State University.

When to Begin Preparing for the Job Search

Time is of the essence for a successful job search. Seniors find it very easy to delay and not devote enough time to their job hunting efforts. It's not too early to start planning your job search when you return to college in the fall of your senior year. Take an inventory of everything it will take to carry out your job campaign. Identify the procedures you intend to follow when carrying out your objectives. For example, the best avenues to pursue for getting job leads; the placement office operations; employer lists; personal contacts and networking; references; completing credentials; scheduling time for interviews; seeking faculty and other contacts' advice; attending workshops; planning a self-marketing strategy; attending professional conferences; and studying the competition and the job market at large.

By completing your homework in advance, you can prepare to enter a full-blown job search about five to six months before you graduate. You will also avoid the last minute stress of many college graduates by having a well-organized plan in mind.

Things to Do Before an Interview

Research Prospective Employers

You know how you feel when an employer knows about you and your background; you feel flattered when they show a special interest in you. The same is true for an employer. By knowing a company's products, financial condition, job opportunities, growth pattern and organization, you are reflecting a special interest and enthusiasm for the employer. An absence of this knowledge can reflect negatively on your application, especially if your competition has done homework.

Once you have this information be sure to relate it to your interests, background and experience, and be sure to let the employer know there is a good match between their needs and your qualifications.

Sources for researching employers can be found in your career information center or library. Company profiles are available in the *National Association of Colleges and Employers Job Choices* or *Peterson's Annual* guides. *Dun and Bradstreet* and *Standard and Poor's* also have much helpful information on various organizations. Check your local reference librarian for a wealth of information in the areas that interest you.

Researching an employer can play a substantial role in making an interview successful. This knowledge will provide you with the opportunity to speak intelligently to the recruiter. Furthermore, this knowledge can tell you if this is an organization you *don't* want as your new employer.

Plenty of effort is necessary to properly complete this task, but all the effort is well worth it, since the prospective employer is duly impressed with your presentation, and you are very familiar with the situation you face with this prospective employer.

Here are some questions to ask yourself in order to decide if a company is really for you:

1. What does this job involve?
2. Does the culture of the employer fit my personality?
3. Are these the kind of people with whom I would enjoy working?
4. Will I enjoy the work?
5. Will this job interfere with my family?
6. Is the company financially sound?
7. Is this the geographical area I want?
8. Does the job fit my long-range goals?
9. Do I feel good about accepting the offer?
10. Will I have adequate training?
11. Are the work hours reasonable?
12. Is the commuting distance reasonable?
13. Does my family think this offer is a good one?
14. Is there another place available where I could do better?
15. Is the salary adequate?

Clear References with Faculty and Others

A minor task, but a thoughtful and wise one, is to let people know you would like to use them as a reference. It alerts them to possible calls and affords you the opportunity to brief them about your interest—which can strengthen the reference's response. It is good to send references a copy of your resume so they will be able to speak accurately and knowledgeably about you.

Study Job Descriptions and Relate Your Background to the Job

Always try to get a job description for any job you are seeking. This gives you a target when writing a resume. It also helps you focus during the interview. This information provides you with an opportunity to explain the match of your education, experience, and interests with the employer's position.

Many interviews end with the candidate diluting the thrust of his or her efforts by focusing on a nonexistent vacancy. By knowing the duties and responsibilities of an available job, you can relate to the needs of the employer more explicitly.

Practice Interview Techniques

It is a good idea to practice interviewing with a fellow student or in workshop practice sessions before getting that all-important first job interview. Many students prepare for interviewing by taking interviews with employers who interest them very little or an organization with whom they have little chance of landing a job. After these practice interviews, they can then approach their prime prospects. Having experience with several interviewers helps the novice hone interviewing skills. In fact, many employers feel that graduating students become more capable at their interviewing skills as the recruitment season progresses. Practice makes perfect.

Interviewers vary greatly in their methods, so don't expect a similar format from each one. When practicing, adopt the frame of mind that you are on equal footing with the interviewer. Confidence is important to a successful interview and practice can help you develop that confidence. You will find that interviewers are human, just like you.

When practicing try to be succinct in your responses since, in the campus interview especially, you have limited time to present your case—generally 20 to 30 minutes. Learn to focus on your strengths and articulate those capabilities.

Practice can also help keep you from floundering when confronted with a question pertaining to a liability. Know, for example, how you will handle questions regarding a low grade point average, if that is your situation.

Do's and Don'ts

In addition to being prepared for interview questions coming from any direction, here are a few do's and don'ts for any interviewing situation:

Do:

1. Be on time.

2. Be neat and properly dressed.

3. Bring extra copies of your resume to the interview.

4. Practice interviewing.

5. Study potential questions and your probable answers to them before interviewing.

6. Know your travel and location restrictions, if any.

7. Analyze your strengths and be sure the interviewer is aware of them before completing the interview.

8. Know your overall and your major grade point averages.

9. Know the market for a person with your talents and be realistic in your salary demands.

10. Know your military status.

11. Advise the appropriate people you would like to use them for references.

12. Be prepared to answer questions pertaining to drugs and alcohol.

13. Be positive in your responses.

14. Respect subordinates of the individual conducting the interview.

15. End the interview with an expected course of action.

16. Thank the interviewer.

17. Keep a record of all interviews conducted.

18. Write a follow-up thank you letter.

19. Recognize that you may receive some rejections but do not let this damage your enthusiasm.

20. Consider all potential job leads and do not limit your efforts to placement services interviews (include networking, newspaper advertisements, directories, etc.).

21. Be straightforward.

22. Take the initiative if an employer doesn't follow up as agreed to in an interview.

23. Remember that *you* are the one responsible for getting a job—don't rely on others.

24. If you want a drink at lunch or dinner or during a reception with an employer, stay with a light drink.

25. Listen intently.

26. Remember that you can negotiate.

27. Be honest.

28. Be professional.

29. Follow up, on time, with everything you say you will do.

Don't:

1. Be a threat to the interviewer.

2. Be late or too early for your appointment.

3. Dwell on your liabilities.

4. Discuss controversial subjects.

5. Be a name-dropper.

6. Interrupt.

7. Make a decision to accept the job immediately upon getting an offer.

8. Accept an offer before you have completed all of your interviews.

9. Renege on a job offer.

10. Smoke unless the interviewer smokes.

11. Take other people with you to the interview.

12. Use profanity.

13. Be overbearing.

14. Condemn former employers, faculty, or associates.

15. Place too much emphasis on salary and benefits at the beginning of an interview.

16. Present a poor resume.

17. Be negative.

Additional Tips When Interviewing

During the course of the interview there are little responses that can sometimes make a difference and strike a positive chord with the interviewer.

When responding to a question, try to relate your course work or work experience to the question whenever appropriate. For example, if you have prepared a term paper related to a given question, work that into your response.

Leadership skills should be accented in your response, if appropriate. Relating some of your leadership responsibilities to a given job can have a very positive effect. If you have worked on team projects make sure that is known. If you have assumed special responsibilities, such as a Multiple Sclerosis Drive that you chaired, bring that into the conversation.

Anything that demonstrates sound work habits, dependability, or perseverance add to the credentials that aren't on your resume and may be pursued by the interviewer. Respond to questions positively. Beware of taking a negative approach in any response.

If you have attended seminars or conferences that have a particular relationship to the job you are seeking, bring those up. Faculty associations that were particularly valuable can be mentioned. If you had any mentors, you might want to mention them.

Give the impression that you want to continue learning by going to grad school while on the job, attending professional meetings, or subscribing to certain journals to indicate your professional approach to your career.

Don't be afraid to express your ideas as they pertain to the job. Stay away from religious, political, and controversial subjects.

Convey the fact that you are realistic in your career aspirations and that you are looking for that employer who is fair and has opportunities for those willing to contribute.

Most recruiters subscribe to the theory that past behavior, performance, and achievement are the best indicators of future behavior, performance, and achievement. Once you recognize and accept this approach by the recruiter, you will respond to interview questions with this in mind.

Coupling this with any advance information you acquire on the job description, company, products, and recent media information (mergers, profit picture, etc.) can make a difference in your responses. The main idea, then, is to relate your background and education to those factors. This does not mean you mislead or misstate your qualifications. It means you relate your background and experiences to what the recruiter is looking for.

Some Special Considerations

How Do Employers View the Grade Point Average?

How to handle questions regarding grade point average (GPA) is a common problem for many students. According to employers, GPAs are merely one of many factors of success on the job. Other important factors in their evaluations were how well-balanced the individual was and the total college experience. Some organizations have a minimum of 3.0 (on 4.0 scale). Public accounting firms seem to put more emphasis on GPA than other areas of employment. Many organizations in the technical disciplines believe there is a high correlation between GPA and intelligence according to the survey. In sales and personnel, high grade point averages have not been an accurate measure of success according to many employers.

My personal experience in seeing students with high and low GPAs is that there is little correlation between GPA and success in business. Quality of the institution is often more significant than GPA. A GPA at one college or university may be an entirely different standard from that of another institution. Departments within colleges have different criteria for giving grades as do professors within a given department.

If you are going to pursue an advanced degree in medicine, law, higher education, or high tech occupations, a high GPA is a decided advantage for admittance to a graduate program. For graduating seniors planning to enter the employment market there are many other factors that are important when employers make their hiring decision. For example, people skills are very important in almost any field you choose (most people who are terminated from a job are terminated for lack of people skills rather than for lack of technical skills). Common sense, appreciation of the work ethic, good written and spoken skills, motivation, integrity, and problem solving skills all are important.

There have been numerous surveys on GPA and future success on the job. Some employers have found that there is a correlation between success on the job and GPA but many others have found there to be no correlation between the two. The larger technical corporations, in my experience, put more emphasis on the importance of GPA than the smaller and non-technical ones.

If you have a low GPA and find you are rejected by an employer because of that reason, don't worry. There are plenty of other employers who will be happy to consider you for the other skills. Many students fear that a low GPA will jeopardize their job opportunities and that translates into lack of confidence in the interview. Don't let this happen to you.

What about Students Who Have Military Reserve Status?

Most organizations have policies with guaranteed employment for military reservists who are activated during a national emergency. Some employers are not aware of federal laws covering this situation. Should this become a subject of discussion in an interview, refer to Chapter 43 of the U.S. Code, Title

38, which states that reservists and national guard personnel who are called to active duty during a national emergency have "protected status." This law is also known as the Military Leave Act.

Transferable Skills

Most graduating students are not acutely aware of the transferable skills they possess, primarily because they have not studied them nor thought enough about them. These skills can be important elements when convincing interviewers of your competencies to handle a given job. To accomplish this task, you might make a list of all the skills you have learned in your various work, volunteer, and educational experiences. For example, you might list supervision of others, managing funds, leadership of teams, sales and marketing skills, solving problems, relating to others, making presentations, delegating responsibilities, meeting deadlines, developing schedules, negotiating with unions, preparing reports, writing letters, preparing speeches, etc. All avenues of communications are important—speaking, writing, conversation, interviewing, and listening. Other skills might include computer literacy, teaching, and organizing tasks. The list is endless.

Responding to employer questions regarding your transferable skills with examples that are not always evident from your work experiences or education can make a great difference in landing a job.

Should You Accept a Job for Which You Are Overqualified?

Some employers say this may be the only way into some organizations. This can be especially true in times of a recession or for students in low demand disciplines. The answer depends on your financial status, your interests, your potential, and the potential of the job offer. The fact is, many graduates are overqualified for their initial positions.

Employers say high performers will be recognized in the long run once they demonstrate their abilities and willingness to work. Many organizations have policies of promoting only from within. Since vacancies are not generally open to the public, this is the only way, sometimes, to join a company. Moving within a company usually is much easier than coming in from an outside organization.

Traditionally, some majors in communication arts, marketing, fisheries and wildlife, advertising, tourism, history, romance languages, and other disciplines have found it advantageous to accept a job for which they are overqualified.

For many, it beats having no job at all!

What If You're Not a "Perfect" Candidate?

In this country, if you are willing to work and respect the work ethic you can succeed. You can be lacking in many skills and abilities, but if you can demonstrate that you want to work and will work hard, there are many employers who will hire you.

Many recruiters feel some college graduates are not willing to "pay the price" the employers are looking for. Employers say too many recent graduates want to start at the top without the requirements necessary to succeed. Some have said the education process has been too easy on them and they have been too protected from making it on their own. Old fashioned ideas? Maybe so, but more and more employers are putting emphasis on co-op programs, internships, summer employment, part-time work (career related), and those factors that indicate discipline and self-reliance.

Another spin-off of these "old fashioned" ideas is that of commitment. Employers believe that commitment to an employer is fading fast. Seniors think in terms of one, two, or maybe three years of working for an employer unless they see themselves on a fast track in the organization. This concept was partially brought about by the rapid growth of business, industry, and government in the 70s and 80s, where people moved upward rapidly if they demonstrated potential. That growth has temporarily been slowed down, thus the vacancies up the ladder are much fewer.

So, when you have your interviews, be aware of these factors when talking with the person doing the hiring. He or she may be just "old fashioned" enough to see the importance of these factors and decide on whether to make an offer to you depending on how you look at these matters.

THE CAMPUS RECRUITING PROCESS

The career planning and placement office is the bridge between the world of education and the world of work. The services offered by universities and colleges vary greatly, but most institutions have basic services such as career counseling, a career library, and the opportunity for on-campus interviewing between students and employers. In addition, many colleges and universities offer workshops, credential referral services, courses in career planning, resume design assistance, alumni contacts, supply and demand information, employer address lists, and starting salary data. Take advantage of these services because once you have graduated and leave the campus, these services are much more difficult to obtain. Personal interviews are particularly more difficult to obtain after you leave campus.

Learn about the Placement Office System

Adequate preparation before the campus interview is extremely important. Talk to the placement director to become familiar with all the services available. Provide ample time in your senior year to schedule interviews. Faculty and placement personnel are excellent sources of information about employers and their needs.

Questions for recruiters should be prepared in advance of interviewing. Some interviewers will ask candidates if they have any questions. At that point, students should be prepared to take the offensive and ask specifics about the employer's job opportunities, organizational policies, and living conditions. If you should be seeking a teaching position, inquire about support personnel, school policies, employment benefits, community support, and living conditions in the surrounding geographical area.

Students majoring in technical subjects will usually find more employers visiting campuses than nontechnical graduates. Liberal arts graduates, for example, may not be able to get as many on-campus interviews as engineers, but liberal arts graduates can find many leads by networking and personal contacts. The career planning library usually has a wealth of information on job search strategies, including interviewing, so avail yourself of those opportunities.

Signing up for interviews can be very competitive. Knowing the rules and capabilities of the placement office operation can sometimes help you get on interviewing schedules that would otherwise not be available to you. Computerized interview sign-up systems can sometimes permit last-minute appointments for schedules that originally were filled. "No shows" happen, and if you know the system, you can sometimes substitute at the last minute.

Meet and Know the Placement Officer at Your School

Knowing the placement personnel at your college or university can be very valuable in your job search and when arranging campus interviews. Personnel in this office can help you handle interviews and answer questions asked by recruiters. They can provide starting salary information and give you an idea of your approximate market value. They can provide reference materials and steer you in the right direction during the on-campus and off-campus interviewing processes.

Sometimes when talking with employers, the placement officer is asked to recommend someone for a particular job. If the placement officer knows you, he or she might identify you as an excellent prospect. Support from friends and relatives can be helpful when finding a job, but quite often, the key person in the recruitment process is the placement officer at your university.

This brings up another important point. Much of the success of an interview is dependent upon the work you accomplish with others *prior* to the interview. Keep key people apprised of your job status during the interviewing process. By doing this, these important people can frequently add suggestions that will help you.

Many students may be reluctant to contact their placement officers, friends or relatives when it comes to the job hunt. They believe they can get a job by themselves—until it is too late. Most people can be contacted and are willing to lend a helping hand to inexperienced job seekers with advice, suggestions, and leads for interviews. This is all part of the networking process that leads to success.

Be Familiar with the Career Planning Library

The career planning library can be a most important source of information. Take advantage of this resource: it is a major element when planning an effective interview. The resources are almost limitless.

Information on file in the career planning library includes a broad range of self-help and job search books in addition to considerable information on job interviewing. Here are a few examples:

Pre-interviewing information on employers can be obtained from company brochures, professional directories, *Standard and*

Poor's directories, *Moody's,* and *Dun and Bradstreet* publications. Nonprint media are also becoming a larger part of career information centers. These include video tapes or laser disc systems plus audio and video tapes on interviewing.

Individual descriptions of jobs, career fields, and industries including supply-demand and salary information (i.e., *Dictionary of Occupational Titles* and *Annual Salary Reports*) are often included.

Self-help materials especially designed for women, minorities, and the handicapped *(I Can Be Anything: A Career Book for Women, The Black Resources Guide,* and *Minority Student Opportunities in U.S. Medical Schools, 1990–91)* can be helpful. Career planning aids *(College to Career: Finding Yourself in the Job Market,* and *What Color Is Your Parachute? A Practical Guide for Job Hunters and Career Changers, 1995)* will get you started (See Appendix A).

Salary information *(National Association of Colleges and Employers Salary Survey* and *Recruiting Trends)* are also available and can help you estimate your economic worth on the job market. It's important to have this information at your fingertips so you better understand your situation and can negotiate your salary needs.

The reference librarian at your library can also be an excellent resource person for finding answers to specific questions to meet your special needs. Your career planning and placement office is also an excellent source for this information.

Take the time to conduct in-depth research on the organizations you intend to interview. Gather as much information as you can on the people, their products, the organization, and its financial health. This information will considerably enhance your employment potential.

Learn the Current Job Market for Graduates in Your Discipline

The job market for new college graduates changes from year to year. Even the supply of graduates changes from year to year (See Chart D).

Chart D
Estimated Supply and Demand for College Graduates (1995–96)*

High Demand/Limited Supply

Accounting College Teaching
Accounting, Professional
Chemistry Teaching
Computer Science
Earth Science Teaching
Engineering College Teaching
Finance College Teaching
Human Medicine (MD)
Industrial Arts Teaching
Learning Disabilities Teaching (MS and experience)
Management Science
Materials Science
Mathematics Teaching
Operations Research Management Science
Osteopathic Medicine (DO)
Physics Teaching (BS, MS, PhD)
School Psychologist/Diagnostician (EdS or PhD)
School Social Worker (MSW)
Teaching of the Emotionally Disturbed

Good Demand/Possible Shortage

Accounting
Agricultural Education Teaching
Bilingual Spanish (with engineering or business as a major)
Business College Teaching (PhD)
Chemical Engineering
Civil Engineering
Clinical Laboratory Sciences
Computer Science College Teaching
Data Processing/Computer Science Teaching
Deaf Education Teaching

(continued)

Chart D

Estimated Supply and Demand for College Graduates (1995–96)* *(continued)*

Electrical Engineering

Engineering Mechanics

Environmental Engineering (Ms, PhD)

Food Industry Management

Food Science

Food: Technology and Management

General Science Teaching

Hotel Restaurant and Institutional Management

Hotel Restaurant/Institutional Management College Teaching

Materials and Logistics Management–Operations

Materials and Logistics Management–Purchasing

Mechanical Engineering

Medical Technology

Nursing (BS)

Nursing College Teaching

Pharmacy

Physical Science Teaching

Reading Instructor College Teaching

Reading Instructor Teaching (MA)

School Administration (superintendent, principal, etc.)

School Coaching (basketball, football, swimming, wrestling, etc.)

School Counseling (MA and three years experience)

School Librarian (MLS)

School Speech Correctionist (MA)

Special Education College Teaching

Systems Science

Teaching the Mentally Handicapped

Teaching the Visually Handicapped

Near Balance/Supply Equals Demand

Administration in Higher Education (housing, admissions, placement, financial aid, etc.)

Agribusiness and Natural Resources Communications

(continued)

Chart D

Estimated Supply and Demand for College Graduates (1995–96)* *(continued)*

Agribusiness and Natural Resources Teaching

Agricultural Economics

Agricultural Technology

Animal Science

Art Teaching

Audiology and Speech Science (MS)

Biochemistry

Biophysics

Botany and Plant Pathology (PhD)

Building Construction Management

Business Education Teaching

Chemistry

Clinical Psychologist (PhD)

Counseling–Agency (MS)

Criminal Justice College Teaching

Crop Science

Dietetics

Driver Education Teaching

Economics

Engineering Arts

English Teaching

Financial Administration

Foreign Language (BA, MA, PhD)/Russian

Forestry

French Teaching

General Business Administration

Horticulture

Human Ecology/College Teaching

Human Resource Management (MBA)

Instrumental Music/Band Teaching

Labor and Industrial Relations (MLRHR)

Landscape Architecture

Marketing

(continued)

Chart D

Estimated Supply and Demand for College Graduates (1995–96)* *(continued)*

Materials and Logistics Management–Transportation/Physical
  Distribution

Mathematics

Merchandising Management

Microbiology & Public Health (MS, PhD)

Packaging

Physics (BS, MS)

Physiology (MS, PhD)

Sanitary Engineering (MS)

Social Work (MSW)

Soil Sciences

Spanish Teaching

Statistics

Teaching English as a Second Language (MS)

Teaching the Physically Handicapped

Telecommunications–ITS option

Urban Planning

Veterinary Medicine (DVM)

Vocal Music Teaching

Zoology (MS, PhD)

Adequate Supply/Some Oversupply

Advertising

Agricultural Engineering

Agriculture/College Teaching

Arts and Letters College Teaching (MA, PhD)

Astronomy

Biological Science

Botany and Plant Pathology (BS, MS)

Child Development

Child Development Teaching

Clothing and Textiles

Communication

(continued)

Chart D

Estimated Supply and Demand for College Graduates (1995–96)* *(continued)*

Communication Arts College Teaching
Counseling Student Personnel Services College Teaching
Criminal Justice
Criminalistics
Distributive Education Teaching
Elementary Education/College Teaching
Elementary Education Teaching
English
Entomology
Family Ecology
Family Economics and Management
Family Studies
Fisheries and Wildlife
Foods and Nutrition
Foreign Languages (BA, MA, PhD) German and Romance Languages
Geography
Geological Sciences
Geophysics
German Teaching
History (BA)
History Teaching
Home Economics Teaching
Human Nutrition
Human Resource Management (BA)
Humanities
Instrumental Music Teaching
Interior Design
International Relations
James Madison (Political Economy, Social Relations, International
    Relations, and Political Theory and Constitutional Democracy)
Journalism Teaching
Microbiology and Public Health (BS)
Multidisciplinary Social Science Teaching

(continued)

Chart D

Estimated Supply and Demand for College Graduates (1995–96)* *(continued)*

Music Therapy
Natural Science College Teaching
Nutritional Sciences
Parks and Recreation Resources
Physical Science
Physics (PhD)
Physiology (BS)
Public Administration
Public Resources Management
Resource Development
Social Science
Social Studies Teaching
Teacher Eduction College Teaching
Therapeutic Recreation
Travel and Tourism Management
Zoology (BS)

Surplus/Substantial Oversupply

Anthropology
Art
Biology Teaching
Conservation and Natural Resources Teaching
Economics Teaching
Educational Psychology (MS)
Family Community Services
Family and Consumer Resources
Geography Teaching
Government Teaching
Health Education Teaching
Human Ecology (General)
Interdisciplinary Studies in Social Sciences
Journalism
Latin Teaching

(continued)

Chart D

Estimated Supply and Demand for College Graduates (1995–96)* *(continued)*

Linguistics
Philosophy
Physical Education Teaching
Political Science Teaching
Psychology (BS, MA)
Psychology College Teaching
Psychology Teaching
Recreation
Religion
Russian Teaching
Social Science College Teaching
Social Work (BS)
Sociology
Sociology College Teaching
Sociology Teaching
Speech/Communication Teaching
Telecommunications
Theatre
Theatre Teaching

Definitions

High Demand/Limited Supply: Appears to be more positions than college graduates.

Possible Shortage/Good Demand: A few more positions than graduates.

Near Balance/Supply Equals Demand: Approximately as many positions as college graduates.

Adequate Supply/Some Oversupply: A few more college graduates than positions.

Surplus/Substantial Oversupply: Many more college graduates than positions.

* Estimated by John D. Shingleton, Director Emeritus, and L. Patrick Scheets, PhD, Director, Collegiate Employment Institute, Michigan State University, 1995.

There has been a prevailing view by some recent college graduates that once you receive a degree the jobs are there for the taking. However, thousands of graduating students have found this to be a myth. Regardless of the year in which you graduate, there is substantial competition, especially in the lesser demand disciplines such as liberal arts, communications, social sciences, advertising, philosophy, and religion.

The important point is this: you are *one* person who needs *one* job. Learn all you can about your competition and the job market, develop a positive attitude, be persistent, properly develop your job campaign strategies—and you will find your way.

The pattern of academic majors in demand among college graduates seeking employment over the past decade has been relatively unchanged.

Health careers over the next decade will offer enormous opportunities due to an aging population requiring more hospitalization and health care services. This occupational area has the potential for the fastest growth according to the U.S. Department of Labor statistics. The second fastest growing occupation requiring a skill is computer programming, which has spin-off applications in other areas of employment, such as accounting and engineering. Demand for engineers will not diminish greatly, in the long run, even though demand fluctuates from year to year.

Education, mathematics, protective services, architecture, and communication technologies majors will usually have job opportunities, but graduates in these majors will have to work at their job hunting to be successful.

As would be expected, new graduates in health services, technical fields, and science majors are expected to receive the highest starting salaries. Engineers, for example, will average about $36,000 a year to start in 1995–96. At the other end of the spectrum, advertising, retailing, telecommunications, human ecology, natural resources, and journalism majors will find starting salaries, on average, in the $18,500 to $22,000 range.

When interviewing with prospective employers, there are many factors that go into a successful interview. A very important matter is understanding the economics of the job market, for this is the reality of the situation.

Supply and demand for graduates varies from year to year. Chart D shows the estimated supply and demand ratios for 1995–1996. This ratio will probably hold for the next two to three years, barring radical economic changes.

Liberal Arts Degree Candidates and the Job Market

Many liberal arts graduates are not aware of the many job opportunities that liberal arts graduates fill. Here is the list of possible opportunities:

Accountant/cost accountant

Administrative assistant/trainee/specialist/coordinator/officer

Advertising account executive

Agricultural marketing specialist

Artist assistant

Assistant account manager

Auditor/auditing consultant

Bank branch manager

Bank development management associate

Benefits assistant

Branch clerk

Business system analyst

Cartographer

Child support enforcement officer

Claims examiner

Collections specialist

Communications assistant

Community banking trainee

Computer specialist/analyst trainee

Contract associate/specialist

Corporate communications officer

Counselor/corrections counselor

Credit representative/analyst

Customer services/relations representative

Direct care worker

Economic development officer

Employee development specialist

Employee relations specialist

Employee trainer

Energy management specialist

Field representative

Financial planner/consultant

Food and beverage manager

Front office manager

Graphic designer

Historical property curator

Human resource officer/representative

Industrial designer

Legal paraprofessional/preprofessional

Management analyst/trainee

Manager/management trainee/associate

Marketing representative/associate/assistant

Museum assistant

Museum education coordinator

Museum exhibit technician

New business clerk

New staff consultant

Office administrator

Operations assistant

Outpatient therapist

Personnel trainee/representative

Photographer

Planning/scheduling coordinator

Police officer

Policy analyst

Private banking representative

Product administrator

Production control analyst

Production management

Production planner

Program supervisor

Programmer/analyst

Project manager trainee

Psychologist

Public relations representative

Purchasing agent

Purchasing assistant

Purchasing/procurement assistant

Quality assurance agent

Quality control trainee

Real estate banking representative

Recreation administrator

Recreation therapist

Regulator specialist

Reliability engineer

Reporter

Reporter trainee

Research analyst/research assistant

Researcher

Residential unit manager/assistant manager

Respiratory therapist

Restaurant assistant manager

Restaurant manager

Retail assistant manager

Retail manager trainee

Sales counselor

Sales engineer

Sales manager/trainee

Sales promotion representative

Sales representative/assistant

Sales representative/trainee

Sales territory manager

Secretary

Securities associate

Scientist's assistant

Senior analyst

Shift supervisor

Showroom trainee

Social services worker

Social work case manager

Social worker

Software analyst

Software developer

Special events assistant

Staff accountant

Statistician

Store manager

Structural engineer

Substance abuse counselor

Supervisor

Supervisor trainee

System analyst

Systems engineer

Tax consultant

Tax professional

Tax services specialist

Technical aide

Technical sales representative

Technical staff assistant

Technical staff engineer

Technical writer

Technician

Territory manager

Traffic coordinator

Transportation specialist

Trust and securities representative

Trust manager

Trust services representative

Underwriter

Unit manager

Video journalist

Water resource planner

Writer

Qualities Sought in Candidates by Employers

It is important to recognize and understand those special qualities sought by employers in order to avoid being turned down for the wrong reasons. Many recruiters, sorry to say, spend a large share of the interview time looking for reasons to turn you down—not a very positive approach to selection of personnel, but a hard, cold fact of the employment process. You may have many glowing characteristics but if there is a flaw to be found that the interviewer finds negative, be prepared to respond with reasonable answers.

Qualities Employers Are Seeking

Many students fear that their grade point average (GPA) may automatically eliminate them. This is true with some employers, but not all. Attaining a good grade point average is important, but most employers are looking for a trainable, well-rounded person with a sound appreciation for the work ethic. This is especially true in many jobs now available in the service industries and government. What motivates a person is also a major factor that most interviewers attempt to find. Emphasis is also placed on the candidate's abilities to not only work with the employers' clients but also their fellow employees. Most employers are looking for "team players" for carrying out the company's goals.

The following are some important characteristics employers seek in a candidate:

Very Important

Overall personality

Honesty and integrity

Enthusiasm

Critical thinking abilities

Written and verbal communication skills

Motivation

Confidence

Appearance

Major (academic) for specialized positions

Negotiating and influencing skills

Potential for given employer's needs

Life experiences

Quality of education

Sometimes Important

Leadership activities

Test results

Extra-curricular activities

Grade point average

Business attitudes

Computer literacy

Final Tips

It is very easy to adopt a cavalier attitude to arranging interviews and finding a job while attending college. There are so many other things to occupy your time during your senior year that procrastination can easily occur.

This has proven to be a big mistake for many college students. Opportunities missed by not signing up for interviews at the placement office or failing to attend career planning events meant employment contacts never arranged.

Admittedly, such efforts require entering an unknown territory, so other activities are given a higher priority. To avoid this pitfall, begin by recognizing that you, and you alone, are responsible for arranging interviews and planning your career. Don't expect others (placement office staff, faculty, relatives, or family) to perform the necessary tasks for you. And, above all, don't expect the job to come to you!

Workshops, Career Fairs, and Employment Seminars

You can learn much about your competition, employers, interviewing techniques, and making contacts by attending workshops, career fairs, and seminars. Talk to employer participants in these events, because doors will be opened beyond your wildest dreams. Be prepared for a quick interview, with a possible in-depth interview later. Through these programs, many placement counselors are assisting in the placement of hundreds of graduates into jobs.

Your Credentials File

Strange as it may seem, many college students do not complete their credentials for a file in the placement office. Sometimes, those who complete the forms are apt to prepare them in a shoddy manner or some forms are not completed to the student's best advantage. Hard to believe? Not really! It happens all the time.

The items in a credentials file will vary from school to school, but all generally contain an official copy of your transcript, an information form, and several letters of recommendation. Your career planning office will assist you in setting up your credentials file.

Let Faculty Know of Your Availability

Faculty frequently meet and talk to employers. These employers often seek recommendations from faculty for jobs that are available. Get to know your professors and make them aware of your availability. You might even talk to them about employment, seek their advice, and leave a resume with them should an employer contact them for candidates to recommend.

Many employers rely heavily on faculty recommendations, and you should, during an employment interview, refer to faculty who would be willing to provide additional information on your college experiences.

The best way to cultivate faculty is to think of them as friends or mentors who are willing to help you. These faculty can be immensely helpful at graduation time with decision-making advice, recommendations, employer contacts, etc. Do not wait until a crisis occurs, however, to seek their help. Cultivate their relationship through course work, seminars, and other meetings of mutual interest as you pursue your education.

THE ON-SITE INTERVIEW WITH PROSPECTIVE EMPLOYERS

You have been screened during the campus interview and found to be a possible candidate for employment, so you are invited to the job site for further interviewing. Prepare carefully for these interviews because you will now be evaluated by your prospective boss and co-workers. Do not assume the job is yours just because you have been invited to visit. Most employers invite more candidates for these interviews than they have jobs available, so they can select from the best candidates.

What to Expect

The on-site interview provides you with an opportunity to evaluate your potential employer, co-workers, job environment, and living conditions. Be sure you prepare a list of questions in advance regarding the whole employment scenario, since it is these interviews that will most likely help you make your decision to accept or reject the job—if it is offered. These interviews may be individual sessions or group interviews, or both. Be prepared for almost anything in these sessions.

Before accepting an invitation to a site visit, be sure all details regarding your expenses and reimbursement are understood. If you are visiting several organizations on one trip, advise them of your plans and suggest that expenses be split among the various employers.

Usually the interviewing schedule is arduous and quite demanding for most new college graduates. Get a good night's rest the evening before the interviewing session. As you proceed with these interviews, think: Would I enjoy working here? Does this organization seem well organized and prosperous? How do the employees and the boss strike me? Try to get into the "culture" of the organization. Attempt to view yourself in this organization with your values, interests, and aptitudes.

The interviewers will vary greatly. Some are trained; some are not. Some seem friendly; some seem officious. Chances are, most of the on-site interviewers will have the campus recruiter's evaluation of you in hand. These interviewers will be more knowledgeable about the organization and the particular job you are seeking, generally, than the campus recruiter; their questions will be more specific and more pragmatic. This is the best time to get solid information on all details of the job, the bosses' expectations, your future potential, your competition, your benefits, and the quality of life you can expect in this organization.

Your schedule during this visit might be something like the one shown in Chart E.

Chart E

Sample Interview Schedule*

ABC Corporation Interview Schedule for
Pat James

TIME	PERSON	TITLE	AREAS TO BE COVERED
8:00 A.M.	Bill Robertson	Employment Manager	Plans for the day. Provide general company information. Explain expense account procedures.
9:00 A.M.	Lois Smith	Supervisor, Production	Explain the job, location, discuss candidate's background as it relates to job.
10:00 A.M.	Frank Beeman	Group Leader	Review credentials and academic work at university. Discuss interest of candidate. Provide information of technical nature regarding job. Review organizational chart especially as it relates to that unit.
11:00 A.M.	Fred Stafford Rita Lopez Ed Fritz	Senior Engineers	Group interview—Questions coming from any of the interviewers covering any subject. Object is to get consensus opinion of candidate from that group.
12:00 P.M.	Lunch–Robertson, Smith, Beeman		To discuss interview to date. Determine how you handle yourself in social atmosphere.
1:30 P.M.	Ann Mooney	Assistant Employment Manager	Tour facilities. Sometimes living areas included in this tour and discussion of schools, housing, etc.
2:30 P.M.	Casius Street	Plant Manager	Opportunity for plant manager to look you over, ask a few questions and make known any reservations he may have.
3:00 P.M.	Bill Robertson	Employment Manager	Make final wrap-up, answer questions, explain follow-up procedure. Discuss general salary expectations, your preliminary interests, and available starting date.
4:00 P.M.	Return home		

* Sometimes tests are scheduled by some employers and are included during the on-site interview.

Kinds of Interviews

After the initial screening interview, which is usually of short duration, you may encounter any one of several interviewing methods during the on-site visit.

One-on-One Interview

The one-on-one personal interview by an employment staff member or line person usually begins the on-site interviewing process. The contents of this interview will usually include your qualifications, the job requirements, and a review of the itinerary for the day. This should be a 50–50 exchange of information and should include both you and the interviewer asking and answering the questions.

Group Interview

In the group interview situation, there will be two, three, or more company representatives asking questions and arriving at a consensus of your potential. It is easy for a recent college graduate to be intimidated in this situation, but relax and be yourself. This format is often used by search committees when seeking candidates for a job. Remember, all members of the group are important. Do not focus your response to one member.

Structured Interview

The structured interview is usually handled by one interviewer, following a prescribed set of questions. This format is used when many interviewers are screening several candidates. This process supposedly provides a uniform set of responses for the decision-makers to consider. Again, be yourself and be honest.

Unstructured Interview

The unstructured interview includes open-ended questions regarding your education and experiences; it is usually free-flowing. During this type of interview, be sure all of your best points are made known before the interview is finished. Not all employer representatives are skilled at interviewing, so a lot of important information can be omitted accidently. In such cases, make sure you cover all the bases; get your message across.

Situation Interview

During the situation interview, after a few preliminaries, the employer describes a situation or problem and asks how you would handle it. Take your time, make sure you understand the question, and respond. If you do not know the answer, simply state that fact or ask for further clarification of the problem.

Stress Interview

The stress interview is precisely what the name implies: a stress/response opportunity. During the stress interview the interviewer(s) asks questions and places you in certain circumstances to test your response to stressful conditions. Once you realize this is the situation, take your time, keep your cool, and play the game.

Visit Your Work Area and Immediate Supervisor

It is not always possible, but whenever the opportunity presents itself be sure to get an interview with your immediate supervisor. The first boss you have is very important to your future success, since this person can place an indelible stamp on you.

Beware of going to work for a person when the "chemistry" is wrong. You can have good rapport with the personnel manager and the campus recruiter, but the key person is your immediate supervisor. A good boss can become your mentor and help you move within an organization and establish yourself.

It is also important to see your work area. Many students have accepted jobs only to find the work environment intolerable, and they have resigned because of this singular reason. The physical surroundings of your work area are important for your enjoyment on the job. Look around the work area before finalizing your plans.

Negotiations and Closure

This can be the most important phase of the interview and requires considerable skill in many cases.

Negotiations

First of all, hear the employer's position thoroughly before you begin to state your side. You may find the employer will offer more than you anticipated.

Next, be sure you understand your bargaining position. If you are the only candidate available for the available assignment, your position is much better than a situation with four or five others possessing comparable qualifications.

Next, come prepared—especially if you expect to negotiate a starting salary. Try to learn the starting salary others have been offered and be sure you know the minimum you will accept. In short, you must negotiate from a sound economic point of view. Just because you feel you are worth more is not an acceptable negotiating position. On the other hand, if you have strong supporting reasons for a higher starting salary, present them.

Understand the total economic package including benefits, bonuses, profit sharing, incentives, travel allowances, and expenses before closing a deal.

Remember, you are in a much better position to negotiate *before* agreeing to employment than you are afterwards. Your bargaining position erodes once you have agreed to be hired.

Closure

Regardless of the interview you have—pre-screening by phone, on-campus, or on-site—always conclude with a course of action that you and/or the interviewer will take following the interview. Too often the candidate leaves the interview not knowing his/her status nor when to expect to hear from the interviewer.

So, at the conclusion of the interview, ask the interviewer about the next step in the recruitment process. The decision may be that "there is no interest on our part at this time but we will keep your resume on file." This is a usually negative response but at least you know where you stand with this employer.

The interviewer may want to refer your resume to various departments in the organization, and then if there is further interest, you will be contacted. You should ask approximately how long will it be before a decision is reached.

If an on-site interview is expected next, request specifics (in writing) so you can plan accordingly.

In short, there are many options that can occur after an interview and you should know the exact actions, and the probable time frame that will be needed. This will relieve you of much anxiety and help you in your planning.

Sometimes employers can lead you into a sense of anticipation, so you relax on your job search only to find that they don't make an offer and you have passed up interviewing opportunities with other employers in the meanwhile. Do not fall into this trap. Keep interviewing until you have an offer in hand and/ or in writing—and have accepted it.

Assuming that you have received an offer for employment, recognize that this is a very important turning point in your career, so treat it with attention. It is also the time when your bargaining position is at its best, and it is critical to your long-term career success.

You should have a good idea of your salary expectations by this time and a clear understanding of the competition for this job. How badly you want the job and how this position fits with your needs, plus common sense, should help you decide what is best for you.

Usually, I do not recommend accepting the initial offer at the moment the offer is extended unless you are sure about salary, promotion, potential, benefits (very important these days), spouse's input, geographical satisfaction, moving costs, training offered, starting date, housing considerations, physical location of the job, immediate supervisor, and time you have to consider the offer. Consider this as a most important decision that can have long-term affects on your future career picture. At the same time, if interested, do not negate your interests in the eyes of the interviewer. One last bit of advice: don't focus too heavily on compensation, if all other factors fit. Lastly, follow through on all your agreements in a timely manner and, if possible, get your final offer and acceptance in writing.

Once you receive and accept an offer you should notify other employers who have made you offers and you should take no further interviews. Your job campaign has come to a successful conclusion. At this time, inform your college placement office personnel of your acceptance of an employer's offer, so they can cease placement efforts on your behalf.

After the Interview

Reimbursement for Expenses

Always have an understanding (how much, which expenses, etc.) of reimbursement for expenses involving on-site interviews *before making the trip.* Most employers reimburse candidates for travel expenses if the employer invites them for an interview away from the campus.

If interviews are arranged off campus at your request and involve expenses, these expenses are usually borne by you. If you are from the midwest and call an employer in New York to arrange an interview, you will generally be expected to bear these expenses unless agreement has been reached on other arrangements in advance.

Some employers reimburse candidates at the end of the day upon completion of an on-site visit. Other organizations reimburse candidates shortly after the visit. Most provide airline tickets in advance, when appropriate. Many employers provide you with a detailed expense sheet to complete and return. In any case, keep close track of your expenses and receipts, and do not pad the expenses.

The Thank You Letter After an Interview

The importance of a genuine thank you letter cannot be over-estimated. The letter should express a sincere, well-phrased appreciation for the opportunity to be considered for a given position.

First, it tells the interviewer of your interest in the job. It also reminds that person that you want to be remembered when making future decisions on candidates. It reaffirms your interest in the opportunity if the interviewer had any doubts of your interest. It also expresses courtesy—too often lacking in day-to-day employment practices.

Thank you letters can be handwritten or typed and should be mailed two or three days after your interview. Mail letters to all who interviewed you.

Keep a Log of Your Interviews

For those having campus interviews resulting in several on-site visits, be sure to keep a log of each interview and maintain a schedule of on-site visits (See Chart F). This will help you keep track of your interviews and action taken at each.

Do not accept "expense paid" visits if you are not interested in employment with an organization. Nor should you accept expenses from two employers if you visited more than one employer on one trip. There have been instances of these events happening, and the student later regretted it, since the employers will contact faculty and/or the placement office staff and complain when this breach of ethics occurs.

Chart F

Employer Contact Log

Date	Contact Phone	Company	Action Taken	Follow Up Date by Me	Comments
1/14	Scott Schultz 371/555–1234	Ford	Campus Interview He will contact me in 10 days	Phone 1/25	Good possibilities.
1/18	Mary Smythe 315/555–3210	Exxon	Campus Interview She will contact me if interested further	Phone 1/28	Iffy.
1/15	Scott Schultz	Ford	He wants plant visit— will set up for 3/16		
1/26	Jim Andrews 517/555–0642	XYZ Steel	Campus Interview		Not Interested.
3/5	Lori Jones 315/555–0610	ABC Advertising	Walk-in visit	None	No jobs!
3/6	Helen Snow 315/555–1212	Growers, Inc.	Walk-in visit. Left Application.		Left application.
3/16	Scott Schultz	Ford	Plant visit 3/23	They will call me in 10 days. Call 3/26.	Looks good

THE OFFER

No matter how thrilled you may be, do not immediately accept a position at the conclusion of an interview. Take at least 24 hours to think over all the terms of the offer. Accepting a job is a tremendous commitment; it plays a major role in the quality of your life and your future. Think of all the ramifications of this acceptance before making the decision. It is one of the most important of your life for it establishes a path that can have lifelong implications.

Also, you should discuss the offer with your spouse, family, or friends to make sure it fits before rendering the final answer.

It is wise to complete all interviews before accepting an offer. However, do not make an employer wait too long for your answer or the offer might be withdrawn. Complete your interviewing schedule. Make sure you have considered all the options before accepting an offer. Do not interview other employers after accepting an offer because reneging on a job acceptance can have serious ramifications, not to mention the embarrassment and stigma attached to such an unethical practice.

Evaluating and Accepting an Offer

On some great day, you may receive a letter something like the one following. Now comes the hard part: do you accept?

Evaluating Your Offer

Some find it expedient to prepare a written index for use when comparing an offer with other job options or with the ideal job they are seeking. A general form can be used for this purpose, to help you give thoughtful considerations to all the key factors in the job selection. A sample evaluation and acceptance procedure follows.

Acceptance Procedure

Once you have made the decision to accept a position, there are several things you should ensure before this job offer is finalized:

1. Be sure the conditions of the offer and acceptance are in order and in writing (See Typical Job Offer Letter). Oral agreements through interviews and phone conversations are part of the preliminary process, but before you complete the deal, it is important that the agreement is in writing. See Evaluating Your Offer(s) form to help you evaluate the offer. See Sample Acceptance Letter to confirm your acceptance.

2. Notify by letter or personally contact all those who have been involved in your job search. Inform them of your job acceptance. This notice should include faculty, friends, placement personnel, references, and appropriate employer representatives who have made job offers so they will know your plans. This is not only common courtesy but a good business practice.

A sample job acceptance letter follows. Your letter should note that you are happy to accept the offer as stated in the notification letter. If you want to counter the employer's offer

Typical Job Offer Letter

ABC Corporation
Box 362
Ivanhoe, Kansas 34620

March 12, 19__

Ms. Jan Schultz
Random Hall
Western State University
Kansas City, Kansas 48814

Dear Ms. Schultz:

Thank you for visiting with us last week and discussing employment opportunities. All of us were impressed with your qualifications and would like to extend an offer to you for the position of Marketing Specialist in our Marketing Department in Los Angeles.

The salary would be $_____ per month and a starting date of August 1, 19__ would be acceptable to us as I understand that is your preferred starting date.

Enclosed is a physical examination form that should be completed by your physician and returned to us as soon as possible. Employment is contingent upon passing the physical examination. You will be reimbursed for this expense.

We will also reimburse you for your moving expenses from Kansas City to Los Angeles, California. A relocation expense sheet for that purpose is enclosed which also includes our policy on payment of these expenses.

It will be necessary for you to let us know your answer to this offer by May 15, 19__, or an earlier date, if possible.

We look forward to having you join us. If you have any questions, please call me at (563) 555–4569.

Sincerely,

John Hopkins
Salaried Personnel Manager
ABC Corporation

encl.

Evaluating Your Offer(s)

Job Evaluation Form		
JOB CHARACTERISTICS	*COMPANY NAME*	*RATING**
1. Do I really want to perform this work?		1 2 3 4 5
2. What is my long-range potential with this company?		1 2 3 4 5
3. Do I like my immediate supervisor?		1 2 3 4 5
4. Is the location right for me?		1 2 3 4 5
5. Is this the best possible job for me at this time?		1 2 3 4 5
6. Does the "culture" of the company suit my personality?		1 2 3 4 5
7. Are there additional educational opportunities available with this organization?		1 2 3 4 5
8. Is my family happy with this choice?		1 2 3 4 5
9. What are the opportunities for advancement (short vs. long run)?		1 2 3 4 5
10. Is the benefit program of this organization adequate?		1 2 3 4 5
11. What is the fit of this working environment with my preferences?		1 2 3 4 5
12. Is the compensation package adequate for my lifestyle?		1 2 3 4 5
13. Other desires or preferences: List: _____		1 2 3 4 5
_____		1 2 3 4 5

* 1 is top rating, 5 is worst

on some point, handle this request by telephone, if possible, so that you sense the response and can negotiate accordingly.

If an employer's offer is made by telephone, repeat the terms of the offer in your letter of acceptance.

Thank the employer for the job offer and express your interest in reporting to work at the specified time and place. Include a paragraph on those aspects of the position that did, indeed, impress you.

Sample Acceptance Letter

798 Chesterfield Drive
Rochester, Ohio 48612

March 10, 19__

Mr. Emanuel Garcia
XYZ Corporation
Atlanta, GA 26412

Dear Mr. Garcia,

This will confirm my acceptance of the position of marketing analyst in the BOC Division of your company. I am delighted with the opportunity to join your organization and feel this matches my objectives precisely. I also feel certain I can make a significant contribution to the XYZ Corporation.

The arrangements for starting work as outlined in your letter of March 6, 19__ are entirely satisfactory. I will arrange for the medical examination and drug test and report to work at 8:00 A.M. on July 3, 19__ as stated. Enclosed are the forms you requested I fill out and return to you.

This promises to be a fine opportunity and I look forward to joining your company.

Sincerely,

Debra Benson

encl.

Special Circumstances

Requesting Delay in a Job Offer

When an offer is extended and you have other possibilities or interviews scheduled, you may want to explore those opportunities. In this situation, you should respond to the offer by explaining your reasons for requesting a delay in responding to the offer. By doing this, recognize that you may jeopardize your chances for employment, although most employers will usually give you a reasonable amount of time to make your decision.

In your response, refer to the employer's communication and the date. State that you are interested in their offer but you:

1. Would like to complete your schedule of interviews.

2. Request that more information is needed to make your decision.

3. Have personal reasons for the request. State the reasons you cannot make a decision at this time.

4. Propose a date for giving them an answer.

5. Request confirmation of this request.

If you discuss this matter by phone with the prospective employer, be sure to confirm any verbal agreements by letter immediately.

Declining an Offer

Being in the position of rejecting an offer requires tact. The matter should be handled courteously and promptly once the decision is made.

Of course, you will want to thank the employer for consideration, time, and effort. Use your own discretion if you want to inform the employer of the reason for declining. Some candidates mention the company they plan to join, but generally, this is not included.

In respectfully declining the offer, you may or may not give the reason(s). Avoid critical comments. Close this letter with an appreciative note and good wishes.

Finally, keep copies of all your correspondence with employers. Retain them for at least a year in case events turn out unexpectedly with the employer hiring you. If that should happen you might like to be considered at a later date by the rejected employer. This is a long shot, but has happened successfully a number of times in the past.

Sample Refusal Letter by Candidate

April 7, 19__

Ms. Shirley Maott
Research and Development Division
ABC Corporation
Boca-Raton, FL 34617

Dear Ms. Maott:

Thank you for your consideration of my employment as an associate research engineer in your company. I have given a great deal of thought to the offer and have decided to decline the offer.

You have a fine organization and there are many aspects of the position that are appealing to me. At this time, however, I have decided on this course of action.

Once again, thanks for considering me and the many courtesies extended.

Very truly yours,

Kristin Mahoney

Thank You Letters

Even though you have accepted a job offer, it is simply good business practice and goodwill to write thank you letters to all the people who have been involved with your job finding efforts.

Be sure to write those employers whom you interviewed with and those who gave you advice during your job search. A note to those you listed as references would be wise also. This thoughtfulness is often neglected but will be appreciated and will distinguish you from other candidates. You may want to use these references or contacts at some time in the future.

When the Employer Doesn't Call

If you do not have a bona fide job offer *in hand*, do not immediately reject any offers. You may find that other offers are not forthcoming and you will not want to burn any bridges until you have accepted a position. If you do, you may be sorry later.

During the interviewing process the interviewer will normally stipulate when he or she will contact you regarding the outcome of an interview. If the interviewer does not contact you by the date agreed, feel free to phone or personally contact that person. Wait two or three days past the stipulated date and then make the contact.

Continue to search for opportunities. Never cease your job search until you have an absolute offer and acceptance in hand. Don't assume goodwill equals an offer. The employment situation can change rapidly in any organization and, until you complete the whole deal, do not discontinue interviewing with other employers.

Closure on the Job Hunt

After the interviews, correspondence, and negotiations, it is a good business practice to have a complete understanding of the offer and acceptance agreement. Such items as job title, job location, compensation, benefits, physical examination conditions (including drug testing), temporary housing allowances (if applicable), expenses (including travel and relocation), potential for graduate school financial support, starting date and time, and a multitude of other details should be received in writing and agreement should be reached by both parties. Many slip-ups occur because of misunderstandings during the interview that can be costly or embarrassing once you start on the job. Having the summary of your negotiations and interviews in written form can prevent these possibilities.

Developing a Career File

As mentioned earlier, job changes are becoming the order of the day and staying with an employer for a lifetime is an exception rather than the rule.

Upon accepting a position, it makes good sense to start a "career file." Periodically through your career, take time to note your various career experiences and milestones. This should include your job titles and descriptions, evaluations by your employer, assignments of special note over and above your regular duties, results of various assignments, and special skills you feel you learned. Also include contacts, associations, offices held, articles written, and speeches given, plus newspaper clippings and professional awards. Finally, include volunteer activities and goals achieved, seminars, conferences, and other educational activities.

You never know when opportunity will knock at your door, so be prepared to enunciate your credentials promptly should an inquiry develop.

APPENDIX A

Bibliography

Billy, Christopher. *Peterson's Business and Management Jobs.* Princeton, N.J.: Peterson's Guides Inc., annual.

Billy, Christopher. *Peterson's Engineering, Science and Computer Jobs.* Princeton, N.J.: Peterson's Guides Inc., annual.

Bolles, Richard. *What Color Is Your Parachute? A Practical Manual for Job Changers.* Berkeley, Calif.: Ten Speed Press, 1995.

Calhoun, Mary E. *How to Get Hot Jobs in Business and Finance.* New York: Harper and Row, Publishers Inc., 1988.

Consoli, Vivian. *Working Smart: A Woman's Guide to Starting a Career.* Glenview, Ill.: Scott, Foresman and Co., 1987.

Davison, Roger. *You Can Get Anything You Want.* New York: Simon and Schuster, 1987.

Figler, Howard. *The Complete Job-Search Handbook: All the Skills You Need to Get Any Job and Have a Good Time Doing It.* New York: Henry Holt and Co. Inc., 1988.

Figler, Howard. *Liberal Education and Careers Today.* Garret Park, Md.: Garret Park Press, 1989.

Knight, Carol Rae. *Interview for Success: A Practical Guide to Increasing Job Interviews, Offers, and Salaries.* Virginia Beach, Va.: Impact Publications, 1990.

Lammon, Katherine R. *Job Search Techniques for Fine Artists: An Advisors Handbook.* California Institute of Fine Arts, 1985.

Levin, Joel. *How to Get a Job in Education.* Holbrook, Mass.: Bob Adams, Inc., 1987.

Linquist, Carolyn Lloyd and Pamela F. Feodroff. *Where to Start Career Planning.* 7th ed. Princeton, N.J.: Peterson's Guides Inc., 1990–91.

Lobodinski, Jeanine, Deborah McFadden, and Arlene Markowicz. *Marketing Your Abilities: A Guide for the Disabled Job-Seeker.*

Molloy, John T. *The Women's Dress for Success Book.* New York: Warner Books, Inc., 1994.

Nivens, Beatryce. *The Black Woman's Career Guide.* New York: Doubleday, 1987.

Scheetz, Patrick. *Recruiting Trends 1994–95. A Study of Businesses, Industries, Governmental Agencies, and Educational Institutions Employing New College Graduates.* East Lansing, Mich.: Michigan State University, annual.

Shingleton, John D. *Career Planning in the 1990's: A Guide for Today's Graduates.* Garrett Park, Md.: Garrett Park Press, 1991.

Shingleton, John D. and Robert Bao. *College to Career.* New York: McGraw-Hill Inc., 1977.

Shingleton, John D. *Mid-Career Changes.* Orange, Calif.: Career Publishing Inc., 1993.

Steele, John E. and Marilyn S. Morgan. *Career Planning and Development for College Students and Recent Graduates.* Lincolnwood, Ill: VGM Career Horizons, a division of NTC Publishing Group, 1991.

You may also want to refer to the following books, available from VGM Career Horizons, for information on job interviewing.

Dr. Job's Complete Career Guide, Sandra "Dr. Job" Pesmen

How to Change Your Career, Kent Banning and Ardelle Friday

How to Get a Good Job and Keep It, Deborah Perlmutter Bloch, PhD

How to Get Hired Today!, George E. Kent

How to Have a Winning Job Interview (second edition), Deborah Perlmutter Bloch, PhD

How to Land a Better Job (third edition), Catherine S. Lott and Oscar C. Lott

How to Market Your College Degree, Dorothy Rogers and Craig Bettinson

How to Move from College into a Secure Job, Mary Dehner

Job Hunting Made Easy, Patty Marler and Jan Bailey Mattia

Job Interviews Made Easy, Patty Marler and Jan Bailey Mattia

Joyce Lain Kennedy's Career Book (second edition), Joyce Lain Kennedy

VGM's Complete Guide to Career Etiquette, Mark Satterfield

B

BUSINESS AND FINANCIAL DIRECTORIES

Career and corporate directors can help the job seeker identify possible employers. A list of some of the directories follows. Consult your local library for additional sources.

Career Employment Opportunity Directory
Ready References Press
Box 5169
Santa Monica, CA 90405

Published in four volumes: (1) Liberal Arts and Social Sciences, (2) Business Administration, (3) Engineering, (4) Sciences. Contains listings of companies currently hiring. Listings include employment opportunities, locations, and special programs.

Directory of Career Training & Development Programs
Ready Reference Press
Box 5169
Santa Monica, CA 90405

Lists management and executive training programs. List includes name, program title and purpose, number of people selected, type of training, qualifications, selection process, name and address of person to contact.

The Directory of Corporate Affiliations
National Register Publishing Co.
3004 Glenview Road
Wilmette, IL 60091

Includes profiles of over 4,000 U.S. companies, including subsidiaries, divisions, and affiliates.

Dun's Million Dollar Directory
Dun and Bradstreet
1 Pennsylvania Plaza
New York, NY 10013

The top 50,000 companies of the 160,000 listed in the *Million Dollar Directory*. Listings include address, phone number, executive names, titles, and statistics.

Dun and Bradstreet's Reference Book of Corporate Management
99 Church Street
New York, NY 10013

Includes biographies of executives of top U.S. companies.

Moody's Industrial Manual
Moody's Investor Service, Inc.
99 Church Street
New York, NY 10013

Lists 3,000 companies on New York or American Stock Exchanges plus some international companies. Includes address, phone number, and statistics. Moody's also publishes directories on bank & finance, public utilities, transportation, and municipals.

Encyclopedia of Associations
Gale Research Co.
Book Tower
Detroit, MI 48226

Published in several volumes. Lists over 20,000 associations alphabetically by industry. An excellent kick-off point for networking. Available on line in DIALOG.

Standard and Poor's Register of Corporations, Directors and Executives
Standard and Poor's Corporation
345 Hudson Street
New York, NY 10014

Includes a massive list of corporations (45,000) and over 400,000 corporate officials. Volume 2 contains biographies of 75,000 executives and directors.

Career Placement Registry
302 Swan Avenue
Alexandria, VA 22301

Resume listing service. Cost is $12 for students, $45 for people in $40,000-and-up range.

About the Internet

Braun, Eric E. *The Internet Directory.* New York: Fawcett Columbine, 1994.

Carroll, Jim and Rick Broadhead. *Canadian Internet Handbook.* Scarborough, Ont.: Prentice Hall Canada, 1994.

Cronin, Mary J. *Doing Business on the Internet: How the Electronic Highway Is Transforming American Companies.* New York: Van Nostrand Reinhold, 1994.

Dern, Daniel P. *The Internet Guide for New Users.* New York: McGraw-Hill, 1994.

Ellsworth, Jill. *The Internet Business Book.* New York: Wiley, 1994.

Estrada, Susan. *Connecting to the Internet: A Buyer's Guide.* 1st ed. Sebastopol, CA: O'Reilly & Associates, Inc., 1993.

Falk, Bennett. *The Internet Roadmap.* San Francisco: Sybex, 1994.

Fisher, Sharon. *Riding the Internet Highway.* Carmel, IN.: New Riders Publishing, 1993.

Fraase, Michael. *The Mac Internet Tour Guide: Cruising the Internet the Easy Way.* 1st ed. Chapel Hill, NC: Ventana Press, 1993.

Gaffin, Adam. *Everybody's Guide to the Internet.* Cambridge, Mass.: MIT Press, 1994.

Gilster, Paul. *Finding It on the Internet: The Essential Guide to Archie, Veronica, Gopher, WAIS, WWW (including Mosaic), and other Search and Browsing Tools.* New York: Wiley, 1994.

Heslop, Brent D. *The Instant Internet Guide: Hands-on Global Networking.* Reading, Mass.: Addison-Wesley, 1994.

Kehoe, Brendan P. *Zen and the Art of the Internet: A Beginner's Guide.* Englewood Cliffs, NJ: PTR Prentice hall, 1993.

Kennedy, Joyce Lain and Thomas J. Morrow. *Electronic Job Search Revolution.* New York: John Wiley & Sons Inc., 1993.

Kennedy, Joyce Lain. *Hook Up Get Hired!* New York: John Wiley & Sons Inc., 1995.

Kent, Peter. *The Complete Idiot's Guide to the Internet.* Indianapolis, IN: Alpha Books, 1994.

Krol, Ed. *The Whole Internet: User's Guide & Catalog.* Sebastopol, CA.: O'Reilly & Associates, 1992.

Lambert, Steve. *Internet Basics: Your Online Access to the Global Electronic Superhighway.* 1st ed. New York: Random House Electronic Publishing, 1993.

LaQuey, Tracy L. *The Internet Companion: A Beginner's Guide to Global Networking.* Reading, Mass.: Addison-Wesley, 1993.

Levine, John R. *The Internet for Dummies.* San Mateo, Calif.: IDG Books, 1993.

Maxwell, Christine and Jan Grycz Czeslaw. *New Riders' Official Internet Yellow Pages.* Indianapolis, IN.: New Rider Publishing, 1994.

Newby, Gregory B. *Directory of Directories on the Internet: A Guide to Information Sources.* Westport: Meckler, 1994.

Persson, Eric. *NetPower Resource Guide to Online Computer Service: Using Online Information for Business, Education & Research;* with contributions by Linda Tsantis, Barbara Kurshan. Lancaster, PA: Fox Chapel Publishing, 1993.

Pike, Mary Ann. *The Internet Quickstart.* Indianapolis, IN.: Que Corporation, 1994.

Quarterman, John S. *The Internet Connection: System Connectivity and Configuration.* Reading, Mass.: Addison-Wesley, 1994.

Resnick, Rosalind. *The Internet Business Guide: Riding the Information Superhighway to Profit.* 1st ed. Indianapolis, IN: Sams Publishing, 1994.

Sachs, David. *Hands-on Internet: A Beginning Guide for PC Users.* Englewood Cliffs, N.J.: PTR Prentice Hall, 1994.

Smith, Richard J. and Mark Gibbs. *Navigating the Internet.* Indianapolis, IN: Sams, 1993.

Snell, Ned. *Curious about the Internet?* Indianapolis, IN: Sams, 1995.

Wiggins, Richard W. *The Internet for Everyone: A Guide for Users and Providers.* New York: McGraw-Hill, 1995.

VGM CAREER BOOKS

CAREER DIRECTORIES
Careers Encyclopedia
Dictionary of Occupational
  Titles
Occupational Outlook
  Handbook

CAREERS FOR
Animal Lovers
Bookworms
Computer Buffs
Crafty People
Culture Lovers
Environmental Types
Film Buffs
Foreign Language Aficionados
Good Samaritans
Gourmets
History Buffs
Kids at Heart
Nature Lovers
Night Owls
Number Crunchers
Plant Lovers
Shutterbugs
Sports Nuts
Travel Buffs

CAREERS IN
Accounting; Advertising;
Business; Child Care;
Communications; Computers;
Education; Engineering;
the Environment; Finance;
Government; Health Care;
High Tech; Journalism; Law;
Marketing; Medicine;
Science; Social &
Rehabilitation Services

CAREER PLANNING
Admissions Guide to Selective
  Business Schools
Beating Job Burnout
Beginning Entrepreneur
Career Planning &
  Development for College
  Students & Recent Graduates
Career Change

Careers Checklists
Cover Letters They Don't
  Forget
Executive Job Search Strategies
Guide to Basic Cover Letter
  Writing
Guide to Basic Resume Writing
Guide to Temporary
  Employment
Job Interviews Made Easy
Joyce Lain Kennedy's Career
  Book
Out of Uniform
Resumes Made Easy
Slam Dunk Resumes
Successful Interviewing for
  College Seniors
Time for a Change

CAREER PORTRAITS
Animals	Nursing
Cars	Sports
Computers	Teaching
Music	Travel

GREAT JOBS FOR
Communications Majors
English Majors
Foreign Language Majors
History Majors
Psychology Majors

HOW TO
Approach an Advertising
  Agency and Walk Away with
  the Job You Want
Bounce Back Quickly After
  Losing Your Job
Choose the Right Career
Find Your New Career Upon
  Retirement
Get & Keep Your First Job
Get Hired Today
Get into the Right Business
  School
Get into the Right Law School
Get People to Do Things Your
  Way
Have a Winning Job Interview

Hit the Ground Running in
  Your New Job
Improve Your Study Skills
Jump Start a Stalled Career
Land a Better Job
Launch Your Career in TV
  News
Make the Right Career Moves
Market Your College Degree
Move from College into a
  Secure Job
Negotiate the Raise You
  Deserve
Prepare a Curriculum Vitae
Prepare for College
Run Your Own Home Business
Succeed in College
Succeed in High School
Write a Winning Resume
Write Successful Cover Letters
Write Term Papers & Reports
Write Your College Application
  Essay

OPPORTUNITIES IN
This extensive series provides
detailed information on nearly
150 individual career fields.

RESUMES FOR
Advertising Careers
Banking and Financial Careers
Business Management Careers
College Students &
  Recent Graduates
Communications Careers
Education Careers
Engineering Careers
Environmental Careers
50 + Job Hunters
Health and Medical Careers
High School Graduates
High Tech Careers
Law Careers
Midcareer Job Changes
Sales and Marketing Careers
Scientific and Technical Careers
Social Service Careers
The First-Time Job Hunter

VGM Career Horizons
a division of *NTC Publishing Group*
4255 West Touhy Avenue
Lincolnwood, Illinois 60646–1975